STRANGE
BUT
TRUE

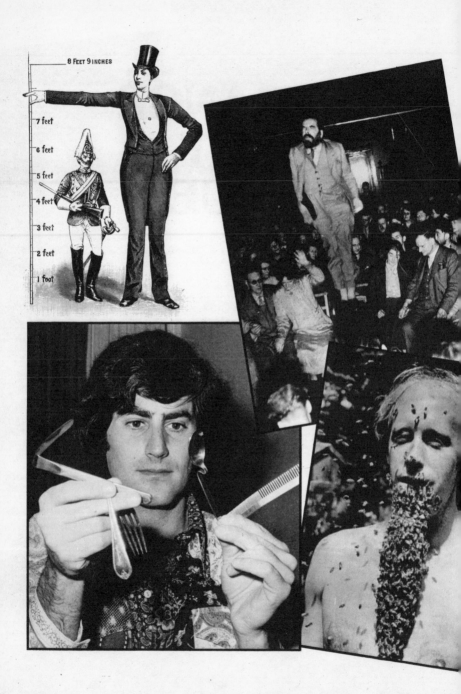

8 FEET 9 INCHES

7 feet

6 feet

5 feet

4 feet

3 feet

2 feet

1 foot

STRANGE BUT TRUE

Edited by
Tim Healey

First published 1983
by Octopus Books Limited
59 Grosvenor Street
London W1

© 1983 Octopus Books Limited

ISBN 0 7064 1967 7

Printed in Hong Kong

Contents

Acknowledgments

The bulk of this book was compiled from newspaper reports consulted at the Bodleian Library in Oxford and the British Museum Newspaper Library in Colindale. I am grateful to the staff of both for their uncomplaining efforts in dealing with some very heavy volumes. Additionally, I have used my own files of off-beat newspaper cuttings.

It is not possible to catalogue here all of the newspapers referred to. Listed alphabetically, the main present-day publications include: the *Daily Express*, the *Daily Mail*, the *Daily Mirror*, the *Daily Telegraph*, the *Guardian*, the *Illustrated London News*, *Nature*, *New Scientist*, the *News of the World*, *Newsweek*, *The New York Times*, *The Observer*, the *Scientific American*, the *Sun*, the *Sunday Express*, the *Sunday Mirror*, the *Sunday People*, the *Sunday Telegraph*, the *Sunday Times*, *Time*, *The Times* and the *Washington Post*. I have found the annual index to *The Times* an especially fruitful starting point for research.

I have traced a few of the accounts through Christopher Logue's *Bumper Book of True Stories* (Private Eye Publication and also obtained newspaper references from Francis Hitching's *The World Atlas of Mysteries* (Collins, 1978) and Peter Haining's *Ancient Mysteries* (Sidgwick and Jackson, 1977).

I have consulted the *Guinness Book of Records* (1982 edition) for some background material, and used other books for the same purpose, notably: Charles Fort's *The Book of the Damned* (Abacus, 1973), Angus Hall's *Strange Cults* (Aldus/Jupiter, 1976), E.S. Turner's *The Shocking History of Advertising!* (Michael Joseph, 1952), *Patent Applied For*, by Coppersmith and Lynx (Co-ordination, 1949) and J.S. Curl's *The Victorian Celebration of Death* (David and Charles, 1972).

Finally, I have included some newspaper extracts contained in the following excellent anthologies: H.L. Mencken's *Americana* (Hopkinson, 1925, 1926), George Ives's *Man Bites Man* (Penguin, 1981), and *This England*, edited by Michael Bateman, (Penguin, 1969).

The publishers would like to thank the following individuals and organisations for their kind permission to reproduce the pictures in this book:

Associated newspapers 25; Bridgeman Art Library 182; Mary Evans Picture Library 135; Tim Healy 2 above left, 15, 37, 44, 77, 84, 90, 91, 113, 159; Barry Fox/New Scientist 116; Keystone Press Agency 63, 169; The Mansell Collection 53, 58, 165, 175; Popperfoto 2 below right, 13, 105; Psychic News 2 above right, 87; Radio Times Hulton Picture Library 107, 181; Royal Geographic Society 141; Syndication International 81; Times Newspapers Ltd 17; John Topham Picture Library 2 below left, 29, 69, 75, 93, 97, 100, 108, 119, 123, 144, 149, 170, 186 above; Wide World Photos Inc. 20, 186–7, 189, 190.

Introduction

THREE HANDICAPPED MONKEYS MUG MOUNTAIN MEN

When the eye is arrested by a newspaper headline like this, who can resist reading on?

From the earliest days of newspaper publishing, the high affairs of church and state, trade and politics, have generated acres of print. Often the passionately debated issues of the past are forgotten today, and interest only historians. But the first newspapers also found space to record more off-beat events: the birth of a four-legged boy, a death by lightning, the antics of a drunken cow, some remarkable medical prodigy. Their fascination is eternal.

Often, weird tales have appeared only as snippets – for example, a man has been found frozen to death, standing upright in a ditch, and the circumstances are briefly outlined. Sometimes the story will so grip the imagination that it demands more extended treatment. Nineteenth-century readers were haunted by lengthy reports of cannibalism on the raft of the *Medusa*, just as in our own century readers have been fascinated by accounts of the Andes survivors.

The weird has featured in the pages of the press just as much as war and taxation. Its essence is hard to define: something perhaps combining the familiar with the unexpected. Occasionally it will take grand or atrocious form: often it will be very low key. Newsman John B. Bogart once defined the difference between the newsworthy and the uninteresting – his remark serves just as well to define the weird.

'When a dog bites a man, that is not news,' he said. 'But when a man bites a dog that is news.'

Chapter
One

Animal Crackers

Bangkok's unemployed monkeys – a dog tried for murder in Switzerland – a hippo's rampage in California – a gerbil drug squad in Canada – the antics of animals are a global phenomenon. What acts of heroism prompted proposals for a London memorial to wartime goldfish?

The Ozark Turkey Drop

Since 1945, the people of Arkansas have flocked once a year to the little town of Yellville deep in the Ozark mountains. The great attraction of this otherwise unremarkable community is its annual sporting event – the Turkey Drop.

Turkeys are tossed from a small, low flying aircraft to glide down to Yellville's central square, where the locals stand ready to give chase. By tradition, the 'plane swoops several times over the little town, and with each swoop, a turkey is released. The event ought to be a graceful and exhilarating affair. Unfortunately, it has not always proved to be so.

Turkeys are not very good at flying and they are not very sharp-witted creatures. With melancholy regularity, they plummeted to their deaths or sustained fearful injury.

In the 1950s, bird-lovers began to object, and the turkey lobby managed to get the rules of the event changed. Instead of dropping live turkeys, the Yellville plane released frozen birds attached to small parachutes – a more humane practice which had unforeseen consequences.

The frozen turkeys, hurtling from the sky, were a menace to property. One smashed through a front porch, destroying the roof. Another badly dented a car. The locals, moreover, had lost the thrill of the chase; the practice of dropping live birds resumed.

Many and various are the horrors which have attended the Ozark Turkey Drop. Once, startled locals saw the first bird fall like a stone, without a single flap of its wings. The man responsible for pushing the birds out of the aircraft had wrung its neck when the unfortunate fowl loosed its own little droppings all over him.

This unpleasant incident was surpassed for grim horror when the local Chamber of Commerce mistakenly bought a batch of turkeys whose wings had been clipped. The discovery was made too late to do anything about it. Not many turkeys survived the 100 foot fall.

In 1981, officials threatened to close down the event, causing much consternation in the Ozarks. Curiously enough, objections had not come from bird-lovers, but from the Federal Aviation Authority which considered the flights over Yellville to be too low for safety. That year, the inhabitants evaded prosecution by using a disguised registration for the 'plane. The subterfuge, however, offered no long-term solution. In 1982 it was decided that the aircraft would swoop down over Crooked Creek, rather than the town square; the drop would be 500 feet.

This worried some of the locals. The *Guardian*, reporting the whole affair, noted: 'They fear that this will give the turkeys time to rediscover the secrets of flight. The 17 birds in the weekend's drop may then glide into the nearby forests for a life of freedom and happiness.'

Almost Human

On 2 June 1971, the *Sun* reported that Iris the Elephant, an inmate of Twycross Zoo, had learned to play *When the Saints Go Marching In* on a mouth organ.

The achievements of animals have always exerted a powerful fascination on humans, and snippets concerning their exploits have long been the staple diet of newspaper readers. Dogs and cats with a special love of Mozart – or of some TV jingle – are so often reported that they scarcely deserve a mention. A more off-beat case was described by *The Times* of 21 August 1982, concerned a musical otter with a particular fondness for the French horn. Whenever musician Henry Merlen practised his horn on the bank of a stream, it appears, the otter swam towards him, climbed onto a platform of weeds, and sat bolt upright to listen intently to bits of Beethoven.

The postwar *Star*, in this context, reported some interesting experiments conducted by snail watchers: 'We have played to them on the harp in the garden and in the country on a pipe,' an enthusiast declared, 'and we have taken them into the house and played to them on the piano.'

On a less exalted level, certain animals have acquired a taste for alcohol. An early example was the case of the drunken cow recorded in the *Illustrated London News* of 17 September, 1842;

'On Friday evening last, a beer-house keeper at Mervhyr put two pails of wort to cool outside his house. A cow, which was grazing close by, went and drank about twenty quarts. It is not known where she spent the night, but early on Saturday she was observed by many running up and down, evidently under the influence of Sir John, and, in the course of the same day, the unfortunate cow died in consequence.'

A sobering tale – and not unique; all the more disturbing therefore that in August 1982, the landlord of the Harrow Inn near Sevenoaks should put down turf in his saloon bar to encourage pets to enter. 'So far,' recorded the *Sunday Times*, 'one horse and several goats have turned up at opening time.'

ANIMAL CRACKERS

A Nation of Animal Lovers
On 18 October 1982, a VIP ceremony was held at Clee Hill near
Ludlow in Shropshire. Here, on the A117 road, Major Adrian
Coles formally opened the world's first cattle-grid with an escape
ramp for hedgehogs.
  The major brought along his two pet hedgehogs to demonstrate
the ramp's effectiveness to his fellow Shropshire county
councillors. Explaining that thousands of hedgehogs die each year
after falling into the grids, the major declared: 'This is a great
day for the creatures. Now I know we really are a nation of
animal lovers.'

Of course, one cannot expect animals to be perfect; they share our weaknesses
as well as our strengths. Particularly distressing is their habit of going around
stark naked; more than one fastidious eccentric has tried to encourage owners to
clothe their pets for the sake of decency. And some animals are frankly
unsavoury in their appearance and habits. In the United States in 1925, the
Yankton Press noted: 'Legislators gathering here have received word that a
representative of the National Association for the Improvement of the
Appearance of Hogs will urge that the appearance of swine should be uniform
and artistic.'

Unsightliness of course is only a minor misdemeanour. In more serious cases,
animals have been brought before the courts. Animal trials have a long
pedigree. In 1499, for example, a German bear was brought to trial for
terrorizing villages; through a legal nicety, the case was delayed for several days
on a plea that the bear had a right to be tried by a jury of fellow bears. In
Switzerland in 1906 a dog was tried and condemned to death for participating
in a murder (its human accomplices, two brothers, were sentenced to life
imprisonment). In Libya in 1974, a dog was tried for biting a human being and
sentenced to a month's imprisonment on a diet of bread and water.

Often, though, animals are forgiven for their failings; and in pet-loving
Britain people have gone to extraordinary lengths to protect them when danger
threatens. There can be few other countries where the following incident,
reported in July 1977, would occur, let alone feature as an item in the national
press: 'Mr Joseph Nash, fire brigade chief, used mouth-to-mouth resuscitation
for 20 minutes to revive a cat overcome by heat and smoke in a cottage fire at
Stroud, Glos.'

A breathless report was filed in June 1980, following a production of a play,
The Last Temptation, at a Cardiff arts centre. The play required that a live
goldfish in its bowl be dashed to the floor onstage. Hardly had the infamous act

American apiarist Mark Kleiber lets honeybees form a beard on his chin

been accomplished, than an RSPCA inspector rushed from his seat, jumped on stage and rescued the gasping creature by popping it into a water-filled plastic bag. He had come prepared – the goldfish survived, and became the centrepiece of an important legal case. In London, two High Court judges ruled that a goldfish was a captive animal and entitled to the law's protection under the 1911 Protection of Animals Act.

If care is lavished on goldfish, what love is expanded on dolphins, those most enchanting and intelligent of creatures? Apart from their exhilarating feats of leaping and retrieval, dolphins have been taught the elements of true communication with humans, doing passable impressions of singing and laughter. Their own vocabulary consists of at least 32 distinct sounds. A dolphin's brain is as large as a human's; it has even been established that the creatures get ulcers when anxious. If any animal deserves the description 'almost human', it is surely the noble dolphin. Small wonder, that when a 350 lb specimen in California swallowed a piece of metal early in 1978, vets took immense pains to relieve the animal of its discomfort. They ruled out using forceps as potentially damaging to the dolphin's internal organs. Instead, they rolled up their sleeves and tried, one by one, to reach the offending article with their own hands. Unfortunately, strain as they might down the dolphin's throat, the metal remained out of reach.

The dolphin was in great pain. The vets at the hospital pondered the problem anxiously. Then they came up with a flash of inspiration. They procured the services of Clifford Ray, a professional basketball player with California's Golden State Warriors. Like many leading practitioners of the sport, Ray had exceptionally long arms – 3 ft 9 in to be precise. Ray reached deep into the dolphin's mouth – and succeeded where the vets had failed. The metal was retrieved from deep inside the creature and and a dolphin's life was saved.

The Magic of Snails

In March 1846, a collection of snail shells from Egypt and Greece was presented to the British Museum. Two of the Egyptian shells were gummed down on a plaque in a display cabinet.

Four years later, in March 1850, a glassy secretion was noticed around the mouth of one of the shells. The specimen was removed and placed in tepid water. After some ten minutes, a snail emerged and began to tour the rim of the basin.

Five months later it was still alive, and, according to the *Annals and Magazine of Natural History*, 'feeds readily, preferring cabbage-leaf to lettuce or any other kind of food yet tried'.

Animals at Work

A mong the forgotten marvels of Victorian invention, one devise caused considerable outcry during the 1870s. This was the dog-driven sewing-machine. The apparatus was marketed and actually used in some English households, employing a special set of wheels which were moved by a little dog on a leash. The dog trotted round and round a movable disc, much as

Sewing by puppy power

asses have moved mill wheels since the dawn of civilization. The Victorians, however, were becoming sensitive to the mistreatment of animals, and the curious apparatus was banned after pressure from the Society for the Prevention of Cruelty to Animals.

The lot of the humble cab horse was exposed at about the same time, with the publication in 1877 of Anna Sewell's classic *Black Beauty*. But the author had a rival in this field, a Californian engineer named Mathewson who was also a passionate lover of horses. Mathewson was worried that the smoke and thunder of the new steam trams were alarming the city's cab-horses. To calm their fears Mathewson devised a special steam tram designed to look like a horse, with a gigantic horse's head mounted on the front. The bizarre vehicle plied the streets of San Francisco for some time, but the commercial failure of the venture bankrupted the unfortunate inventor.

Animals have been harnessed to the needs of humanity in a variety of ingenious ways. In December 1970, for example, it was reported that the United States Navy was testing three particularly intelligent and alert dolphins as submarine trackers to monitor enemy underwater activity in South Vietnam. An interesting sidelight on the report was offered by *The Times* of that month, which described how the story, carried by Reuters press agency, was originally filed in French. Startled news editors first read that 'three black infantry soldiers of particular intelligence and sensitive ear' were to be used in the underwater tests. There followed a correction: 'three black guinea pigs of particular intelligence and sensitive ear' etc. Finally, Reuters got it right, and issued a note of explanation: 'The original French-language text uses the word *Marsouin*. According to the dictionary, this translates as "dolphin", "colonial infantry man" and "guinea pig". Regrettably, we came up with the right translation on the third try only.'

The use of animals in warfare is not new. It was revealed in 1970 for example, that the Germans had tried to destroy Britain's potato crops with beetle bombs. The bombs consisted of containers filled with Colorado beetles, and the first was dropped on the Isle of Wight in 1943; evacuee children helped to round up the beetles.

The terrifying reputation of certain creatures has also been harnessed to the needs of law enforcement. In 1981, for example, two red-kneed tarantulas from South America did service as security guards at a jewellery exhibition in the Bede Gallery at Jarrow.

The gallery owner found he could hire tarantulas from a pet shop for just £5 a month, plus a daily supply of maggot-like mealworms – an enticing charge compared with the £4,500 he paid for human guards at an earlier exhibition. For six weeks, the spiders were encased with the jewellery as a deterrent to would-be thieves. 'Crooks hate things like dogs and spiders,' explained the

Securifear – a tarantula employed to guard jewellery

owner. The pet shop proprietor dismissed the dangers. Tarantulas get to know the hand that feeds them and wouldn't sting unless provoked by sudden movement. The sting itself is rarely worse than that of a bee. Tarantulas are really very friendly – the pet shop had sold four as Christmas presents.

Clearly, Securifear is the coming thing; but it has its disadvantages. In August 1981, a Philadelphia man who carried a python in a bag as protection against muggers was arrested for recklessly endangering another person. The person in question was a policeman. The snake bit the policeman who clubbed it to death with his truncheon.

The *Observer* of August 1982 announced a less alarming development in animal crime-busting. Prison drug rackets in Canada are to be tackled by a team of highly trained gerbils. Selected for their keen sense of smell and trained at a secret government centre, these small mouse-like creatures are to revolutionize the fight against the smuggling of drugs into federal penitentiaries.

The gerbils' potential was developed by the Correctional Services of Canada, a body responsible for the nation's main prisons. Gerbils have already proved their worth in sniffing out drug-smugglers at airports. They have various advantages over tracker dogs, needing little food or space, being relatively quiet, and loyal to more than one handler. The gerbil gaol squad is to be kept at prison gates, trained not only to sniff out various drugs but to press alarm bells if they scent narcotics.

All monkeys are clever, but some are more clever than others. A particular prodigy was Johnnie, a rhesus monkey owned by Mr Lindsay Schmidt, a farmer of Balmoral, Australia. Johnnie could drive a tractor – and turn left or right on command.

Animals are feeling the pinch of the current recession as much as their human counterparts. Consider the plight of Bangkok's unemployed monkeys. As reported by *The Times*, several thousand monkeys in southern Thailand are out of work because of a sudden drop in the price of coconuts, which the animals had been trained to pick. A Thailand MP, who exposed this sorry state of affairs, declared that they normally earned good money for their owners, and had helped to send many local people to universities in Bangkok.

A Strange Gift
**Northampton:- A pickled monkey, which once acted in one of
D.W. Griffiths' pictures, is perhaps the strangest gift ever
presented to Smith College, which has received many useful,
ornamental and historically valuable presents.**
Springfield Republican

Lost Property

I n any catalogue of the world's weirdest novels, *Against Nature* by Joris-Karl Huysmans would find an honourable place. A classic of late-19th century decadent literature, the book describes a nobleman so refined in his tastes that he encrusts the shell of a living tortoise with jewels so that its iridescence will enrich the hues of his Oriental carpets. Fact is no less strange than fiction. Consider the following item, from the *Evening Standard* of 4 March 1929:

'Officials of Imperial Airways today opened a small flat box left behind by a passenger. It contained a live tortoise wrapped in pink cotton wool. The back of its shell was studded with rubies, emeralds and other stones.

'Inquiries revealed that the box belonged to a woman who had flown from Paris to London on the noon airliner on Saturday. No application has been made yet for the return of the pet.'

Fact, indeed, is often stranger than the most imaginative novelist would dare to suggest. A lost alligator was once found on the Southern Railway and an elephant found straying in Camberwell. A porpoise was discovered propped up in one of the cubicles of the men's lavatory in Glasgow Central Station. The staff at first thought it was a dolphin, but the 4 ft, 64 lb carcass was identified as a porpoise by the museum's department at Kelvingrove Park. Nobody knew how it had come into the lavatory. One gentleman told *The Times*: 'We had heavy rain and there was flooding, but this is ridiculous.'

Among the miscellaneous items left behind on LMS trains in 1946 (5,630 umbrellas, a glass eye, a barrel organ, artificial teeth and limbs) were a case of butterflies, a cage containing a two-headed calf, and a three-legged cockerel.

The RSPCA hostel at London's Heathrow Airport has presented the newspapers with much colourful copy over the years. On one occasion a stowaway snail was rushed to the hostel. It was a 7 in molusc of the edible variety, which had hidden on a Comet from Nairobi and Benghazi. On another occasion, a python was found on top of the baggage carousel in the main customs hall. In November 1978, a woman supervisor from the RSPCA removed the snake which earned the nickname of Snoozy, because it was dozing; the snake was transferred to the hostel, where it was treated for a mouth infection. It had been one of those weeks at Heathrow. Earlier a man had caused panic in the customs hall when he was stopped carrying four pythons, four racer snakes, and terrapins in pillow cases.

A Folkestone man had a deeply disquieting experience when he opened a bottle of stout and the head of a 16-in snake popped out. Happily, the snake was dead, but how it had got into the bottle remained a mystery. Equally unnerving was the experience of a Bedfordshire man who bought a chocolate bar at an off-licence. He bit into something hard which he thought was a nut, but when he spat it out he found a mouse's head complete with eyes, teeth and whiskers. The affair came to court. A spokesman for the manufacturers said it was the first case

Bubbles, doped and restrained at the end of her saga

of its kind brought against the firm since it began production in 1831: 'The entire unsold stocks of this particular sweet made on the same shift were recalled and examined, but no other trace of the animal was found. After a most detailed investigation, we think these remains got in via the paper sacks used for transporting biscuits used in making these bars. The system has been changed and the sacks are no longer used.' The firm was fined £50 and ordered to pay £15 costs.

Sometimes, of course, the discovery of an animal in an unusual setting is the result of a deliberate escape bid. 'Ape pole-vaults over park moat', announced *The Times* on 18 July 1978. The head keeper at Longleat Safari Park, Wiltshire, had been badly mauled by a chimpanzee which escaped from an island by pole-vaulting across a park using an 8 ft pole.

The head keeper recovered from his wounds; and the recaptured chimp was put down.

Sad too, was the fate of Bubbles, another freedom-hungry zoo inmate, whose escapade kept Californians enthralled for nearly three weeks in the spring of 1978. During the early months of that year, the weather provided an apocalyptic setting for Bubbles's adventure. After weeks of torrential rain, the hills and cliffs of California had dissolved into swamps of mud and boulder, blocking main roads for miles. A fleet of lorries carrying oranges to market was overcome by an oozing avalanche and spangled the mud with its colourful cargo. A Los Angeles cemetery subsided, so that coffins and corpses slid down the hillside ending up on the back porches of houses. Events reached their climax, however, when it was reported that a 4,000 lb hippopotamus named Bubbles was strolling down a main thoroughfare in Orange County, with almost the whole California Highway Patrol on her tail and the traffic piled up behind her.

Bubbles was an inmate of the Lion Country Safari Animal Park, and had normally been happy enough to remain on the lake to which her keepers had confined her. Perhaps it was the drama of the deluge which had quickened her sense of adventure. Anyway, Bubbles escaped from the safari park and found herself another lake; unfortunately, it bordered a much-used highway where the hippo posed a weighty problem for motorists.

For days, police and park rangers stalked her with tranquillizer guns, and on several occasions managed to hit her with doped darts. Bubbles remained fully conscious and entirely unconcerned. Then, after some 20 days on the loose, Bubbles unaccountably keeled over and died. The cause of death was not apparent and a post mortem was carried out on the body. It is thought that she was hit by two tranquillizer darts more or less simultaneously, with consequences which could not have been foreseen. In all events, the great Californian Hippo Hunt was over.

Mail-Eating Snails –

On 3 October 1980, *The Times* published the following letter from Mr Harry Greenway, Conservative MP for Ealing North:

'Sir, My nine-year-old daughter posted a letter in a small post box in a hedge, deep in the English countryside last month.

'To our surprise, the postman who had collected the letter early next morning brought it to us saying that snails had eaten both the stamp and a large part of the envelope: replacements were necessary, but he would not pay.

'I took the matter up at the local post office whose head postmaster immediately supplied a new stamp, apologized and accepted my offer to pay for the second envelope.

'The snails concerned must have moved and eaten their prey unusually quickly. Has any reader had a similar experience and is this particular gastropod alone in these destructive habits?'

The letter provoked a long-lasting correspondence which persists to this day. Readers learnt, for example, of marauding molluscs devouring computer printouts, and of a notorious letterbox set in a stone post by the shores of the Llyn Llywenan in Anglesey, which was renowned for the voracious appetites of its inhabitants. An especially edifying note on the roosting habits of snails was supplied by a Miss Prudence M.F. Raper. Snails, she wrote, are particularly fond of country postboxes set into ivy covered walls. But Mr Greenway did not need to fear for the safety of his letters if he learned the countryman's snail post code:

'First, establish the presence or otherwise of snails by putting your hand through the slot and feeling around it inside for a knobbly row of shells. Being nocturnal creatures, the snails roost at the top of the box during the day, descending at night to munch their way through any letters posted by innocent townees after the last collection of the day.

When the postman opens the box next morning, hey presto, no snails: they have returned aloft to sleep off a surfeit of stamp gum.'

Readers further asserted that a multitude of snails in a postbox was a sure sign of coming cold weather. More than 200 snails were discovered in Mr Greenway's postbox prior to the hard winter of 1981; the following September, only one gastropod was found to have slipped in for a meal. The postman prophesied a mild winter for 1982.

As a footnote to the saga it should be noted that the winter of 1982/83 was indeed exceptionally mild – the snails got it right.

These Animals are Dangerous

O ne bright spring morning in 1976, Mrs Poppy Hull, an accountant, was strolling to work down Chertsey Road in Woking, Surrey. She felt what she thought was a pair of arms on her shoulders. Mrs Hull turned and saw that it was a lion. She collapsed. The lion stood over her until its owner arrived at the scene.

The lion's name was Shane, and he was the 14-stone plaything of Mr Ronald Voice, who worked for a taxi company in Woking and kept his pet in an old double-decker bus. Mr Voice had been playing with the lion in his back garden when the event occurred. It was not clear why it had approached Mrs Hull, unless it was because she was wearing a leopard-skin coat.

As it happened, Mrs Hull was shaken but unhurt. Shane was quite harmless. The incident merely illustrates the alarm some pets may inspire. Lions, cheetahs, pythons and tarantulas are among the more obviously perilous creatures. But nature is red in tooth and claw, and practically any creature may turn nasty. Reports of savage assaults flood in almost daily from around the world. Consider the following from the summer and autumn of 1982:

Kangaroo Punch (Australia): As Mr Danny Pocock, 59, a train driver, walked to work near Wycheproof, 175 miles north west of Melbourne, a rogue red kangaroo sprang from nowhere and felled him with a series of expert punches. Mr Pocock described his ordeal as 'terrifying, he went up like a boxer and hit me with an almighty thump. He knocked me down three times altogether . . . and I lost all three rounds.'

Pony Excess (West Germany): A girl got a powerful response when she patted a horse in Aaachen, West Germany. The horse sank its teeth into her left breast and wouldn't let go even when bystanders hit it with sticks. The 20-year-old girl finally freed herself by biting the animal on its nostrils.

Three Handicapped Monkeys Mug Mountain Men (China): Police were scouring the slopes of one of China's holiest mountains for three mugger monkeys who, according to the *Daily Telegraph*, had been robbing tourists and pilgrims. 'Each of the three old monkeys has a physical defect. One is hare-lipped, another is one-eyed and the third has only three fingers on its right hand,' the paper said. It appeared that the terrible trio had been attacking visitors to Omei mountain in the central district of China and stealing watches and bags. Tourists were advised to bring food as a bribe to distract the monkeys' attention, making escape possible.

ANIMAL CRACKERS

The mugger monkey headline vies for startling effect with the classic simplicity of the following item, which appeared in the *Star* of 9 July 1948:

Hare Shoots Man – And escapes from car window.
'Johannesburg, Tuesday. – A motorist from East London (South Africa) shot a hare and threw it into the back seat of his car.
The hare was only stunned and, regaining consciousness, touched off the trigger of the gun as it leapt out of the window.
The shot wounded the motorist in the neck.'

Woman Savaged by a Dead Sheep! So far as I know, this headline has never appeared in the national press. The incident was, however, the subject of a humorous note in the *Times* Diary of 15 September 1982. Mr Denis Healey, deputy leader of Britain's Labour Party, had won a certain reputation for colourful abuse of political opponents – in a famous and oft-quoted remark, he likened being attacked by Sir Geoffrey Howe, Conservative Chancellor of the Exchequer, to being savaged by a dead sheep. 'He probably did not think such a thing was possible,' noted the Diary. 'But it is, oh, it is. While cookery writer Philippa Davenport was preparing for her demonstration tomorrow in Harrod's new cookshop, a frozen leg of lamb fell from the top of her freezer and laid her out.' Ms Davenport was badly concussed, and taken to hospital.

While solo assaults by maverick animals, dead or alive, have been the cause of alarm, how much more terrible are mass attacks? Plagues of snakes or spiders are commonly reported in Australia, South Africa, India, South America and elsewhere. More improbably they have also occurred in suburban England. During an exceptionally hot spell in July 1975, for example, more than 200 snakes were taken out of a swimming pool at an empty mansion in Purley, Surrey. The snakes had apparently slithered in to escape the heat. More unlikely still was the great invasion of August 1982, which took place at Burnt Oak, on the northern outskirts of London:

Hamster Horror – Superhamster Feared screamed the headlines. At Burnt Oak, hamsters were taking over. Some terrified residents had to be moved from their homes as hordes of these small, normally timorous creatures infested the council estate at Hook Walk. Hamster shields were set up to protect houses, especially around television aerial lines which the animals used as routes up walls and into bedrooms. One resident, with his son, aged 15, told reporters that they had trapped and killed nearly 200. The council was besieged with complaints.

Hamsters were first introduced into Britain as pets in the 1930s; it was thought that those of Burnt Oak were descended from the normal species but had somehow escaped captivity and gone wild, thriving in rubbish bins, adapting to the harsh English winter. The Ministry of Agriculture was

Horror in Burnt Oak – a hamster peers through a letterbox

consulted and a number of poisons tried – all without success. Experts feared that the hamsters' ability to resist both poisons and cold weather showed that they were on their way to becoming superhamsters. Unchecked, they could spread over the rest of the country, disturbing the food chain and posing serious problems for agriculture.

Barnet council ordered an all-out offensive. Officials came in gumboots, armed to the teeth with traps and bait. But the hamsters were too quick for them. Not one of the furry pests was caught after the campaign began. Zoologists blamed the council's methods; tractor mowers had been used to clear overgrown gardens, driving the hamsters underground. One expert, quoted in the *Hendon Times* said: 'Barnet council really don't know much about the habits of hamsters at all – hamsters burrow several feet down.'

Perhaps the hamsters had moved on to improve their stock elsewhere. Or perhaps they still lurk in secret burrows beneath Burnt Oak, waiting, waiting . . .

Councils have often shown a marked insensitivity in handling pest control. In January 1977, for example, the local council at Henley in Oxfordshire became so enraged at flocks of pigeons depositing evidence of their presence on the Town Hall that plans were made to deport the entire pigeon population of Henley to Yorkshire. Local bird-lovers caused an outcry. So did Yorkshiremen. The proposal was dropped.

Close encounter with a spitting cobra

The spitting cobra is one of the most terrifying reptiles in the animal kingdom. It directs a jet of venom into the eyes of its victim, and can hit its target at a range of up to six feet. The poison is deadly for many creatures, and may cause blindness in humans. In November 1982, a Zimbabwe businessman named Kenneth Hampson had a perilous encounter with one such cobra – and was saved by a mother's milk.

Hampson discovered the cobra in the engine of his car while travelling through the bush north of Bulawayo. As he reached under the bonnet to remove it, the creature spat. Hampson staggered back, clutching at his face. Luckily, however, an African had stopped nearby in a lorry. 'He pushed me over to his wife who was feeding a baby and told her to squirt milk into my eyes,' the businessman said. Hampson was then rushed to Bulawayo general hospital where he was told that the woman's action had saved his sight.

Doctors explained that human milk is an excellent first aid remedy for cobra venom in the eyes. It neutralises the neuro-toxins present, diluting the poison and soothing the pain.

A Real Learned Pig

A famous exhibit at London's Bartholomew Fair in 1833 was
TOBY THE REAL LEARNED PIG, billed as an 'Unrivalled
Chinese Swinish Philosopher.' Toby appears to have been a real
prodigy. It was advertised that 'he will spell, read, and cast
accounts, tell the points of the sun's rising and setting, discover
the four grand divisions of the earth, kneel at command, perform
blindfold with 20 handkerchiefs over his eyes, tell the hour to a
minute by a watch, tell a card, and the age of any party. He is in
colour the most beautiful of his race, in symmetry the most
perfect, in temper the most docile. And when asked a question he
will give an Immediate Answer.'
  Bold claims – but even Toby had his rivals. Also exhibited at the
Fair was THE AMAZING PIG OF KNOWLEDGE who was
credited with the occult power of thought-reading.

The pigeon peril is, of course, merely one of the minor hazards of urban life.
To postmen, and to all who have read *The Hound of the Baskervilles*, dogs are a
much more obvious danger – in bark and bite alike. To restrain barking, some
particularly unpleasant dog collars came on the market in the United States in
1977. The collars gave the dogs electric shocks when they barked; a typical
brand name was Wuf-E-Nuf. Not only were some of them demonstrated to be
cruel to the pets – producing voltages ten times highter than claimed – they
were also inept. The devices could be activated by other dogs barking, car
hooters hooting and hands clapping. Moreover, they could give a nasty shock to
any one who grabbed the collars.

Of course, perfectly normal dog collars can prove perilous to people. A
distressing case occured in New York in August 1977, when a girl aged 16 was
walking her dog on a standard metal lead. She was seriously injured and the
dog died of electric shock when it urinated on a faulty electric sign.

To timid commuters, there are few more disquieting sights than that of a
Very Big Dog on a bus seat facing them. The subject once caused heated
correspondence in the *Nottinghamshire Evening Post*. Moved by the complaints of
one reader, another replied:

'May I say that I am considerably smaller than my German wolfhound. On
the few occasions we have had to travel together upon a crowded bus, it has
proved impossible to stand in the gangway without it being brutally kicked by
other passengers. It has thus been a matter of convenience that the dog have
my seat, and at times on a long journey I have sat on the floor (I have weak
legs). This has invariably made me the butt of much callous laughter, and
such inept comments as "why don't you bring a camel as well?" show the
ignorance of most of the travelling public.'

America's Urban Alligators

One of the most recurrent pieces of newspaper lore about New York life is the story that the city's sewer system is inhabited by hordes of prowling alligators. The alligators, so the tales go, are the one-time pets of wealthy and eccentric New Yorkers who, having grown tired of them, flush them into the sewer system.

The chief of the city's underground drainage and aqueduct system is constantly pestered with enquiries about the awesome, subterranean prowlers. Time and again he has refuted the tales. There are no alligators in New York sewers. No authenticated case of an alligator encounter has ever been reported. New York's alligators are fiction, not fact.

Then, in August 1982, the drainage department was confounded. An alligator was caught in the water system.

Measuring only 26 inches long, she was hardly the nightmare creature of press legend; but an alligator she was, 'large as life and twice as snappy', according to one report. She was snared in a reservoir which supplies the city's drinking water about 25 miles north of Manhattan. An expert told reporters: 'The way to catch the things is to wait until dark and then shine a light in their eyes.'

This handy tip for catching alligators has greater value in America's southern states, where the razor-toothed reptiles are a more menacing presence. Alligators are native to the southern deltas, but until recent years they had practically been exterminated by hunters who obtained high prices for their skins. Then, in the late 1960s, alligators became a protected species – and began to make their comeback with a vengeance. A particularly nasty infestation occurred at Homosassa Springs, Florida, in 1966 and was the subject of much attention in the national press.

By the late 1970s, alligators were becoming a fairly common sight in Miami and other southern cities. They turned up in people's back yards and swimming pools. Once in a while, an alligator would snap up a poodle or other pet. In the summer of 1977, motorists in downtown Miami could hardly believe their eyes. For there, sprawled on a sidewalk at a major road junction, were two quite colossal alligators, apparently waiting for the traffice lights to change.

Cars screeched to a halt amid a riot of horn-honking. The police were summoned as terrified pedestrians raced from the scene. But by the time the police arrived, the alligators had slunk off to the nearest sewer.

Today, alligators have attained the status of major pests, and the skills of the professional alligator catcher are as prized as those of the ratcatcher of the past.

Who's for a dip? Alligators at Homasassa Springs, Florida

Late Lamented Pets

On 13 July 1982, the *Daily Telegraph* carried a melancholy tale. A village teacher in South Glamorgan had fired his starting pistol to demonstrate what pupils should expect on sports day, and the class's pet hamster died of a heart attack.

The British love of animals was already a legend in 1926, when the *American Mercury* intrigued its readers with a cablegram from London reading: 'The Society for the Prevention of Cruelty to Animals announces that it will spend $10,000 to erect a cenotaph at Hyde Park Corner "in memory of the birds, beasts and fishes who gave their lives for the empire in the World War".' The fish referred to were goldfish killed in the gas tests.

In 1978, animal lovers jammed the switchboards at ITN to complain about a news item concerning a cat. It had been read by newsreader Reginald Bosanquet who ended *News at Ten* with a report about an emergency call from an old lady. The incident occurred during a firemen's strike of January that year, and the call was answered by an Army Green Goddess fire appliance in London. Soldiers arrived to rescue the old lady's pet cat from a tree, and with their mission accomplished were invited in for tea. They accepted gratefully, then left.

Unfortunately, they ran over the rescued cat on their way back to barracks.

Concern for cats is by no means a British obsession, however. In February 1978, the newspapers carried a macabre report from California where a critically ill woman was found to be tending 170 dead or dying cats in her one-bedroom flat, placing the dead ones in a makeshift morgue of cardboard boxes. They were found after the woman was taken to hospital. A spokesman for the local animal shelter said that one hundred dead cats were found stuffed in cardboard boxes stacked to the ceiling, in plastic bags and on top of tables. The 70 surviving cats were half-starved.

The truly devoted pet-lover may have a deceased creature stuffed by taxidermy so that its likeness at least survives. Some practical hints on the art were offered by a Lieut.-Colonel Cuthell, late 13th Hussars, in the pages of a 19th-century paper. Although in no sense a news story, the following advice on stuffing birds conjures up exceptionally weird and remorseless scenes:

'*The Head.* – If the head is very much larger than the neck, cut the throat lengthwise to remove the head. It is immaterial whether the eyes are taken out before the head is skinned down or after. The gouge should go well to the back of the eye and separate the ligament which holds it to the socket. Should the gouge go into the eye, it will let out the moisture, which often damages the skin. Some people crush the skull slightly to make it come out of the skin easily, but this I do not advise. Remove the brains by taking out a piece of the skull at the back as you cut off the neck. Pull the eyes out of their cavity and fill up their place with wool soaked in arsenical soap. Anoint the skin of the head and the neck well with arsenical soap, and place in the neck a piece of stick covered with wool, the end of which put into the hole made in the skull for extracting the brains.'

The journal in which these handy tips appeared, incidentally, was the *Boy's Own Paper.*

Fate had something more dignified in store for His Most Gracious Majesty the Lord Grimsby of Katmandu, whose funeral took place in Lancashire in the summer of 1974. For three weeks, His Majesty lay in state on a silken bed. The owner, David Bates of Preston, said: 'The lying in state was just like that of Queen Victoria. He had a diamond ring on his beak, his favourite piece of jewellery and a little crown on his head. There were silver candelabra, palm leaves and other things around him.' At the funeral, the casket was covered with 1,000 carnations. An oration of poems by Shelley and Wordsworth was read.

The *Sunday Times* noted: 'At £1,500 this was probably the most expensive funeral a parrot has ever had.'

Chapter Two

Disorderly Conduct

From murder by exploding cookbook to such minor misdemeanours as roaming the streets in fancy dress, apparently normal people have sometimes behaved in very disorderly ways. A jealous husband propelled himself through his rival's kitchen window from a homemade catapult. An innkeeper murdered his customers with a suffocating bedstead. In a celebrated case of 1951, a whole French village went mad.

Perfectly Normal People

An attorney sat in his Salem, Virginia, office waiting for a client charged with drunk driving. As the lawyer pondered the case he heard an almighty crash. A car ploughed through his front door and came to a halt in the middle of his office. The driver was the client he was waiting for.

Intoxicated with alcohol or rage, otherwise normal people sometimes do behave in most unusual ways.

'The Night the Human Birdman Gatecrashed on the Bard' was how the *Bedford Record* headlined an incident which occurred during an open-air performance of *A Midsummer Night's Dream* at Woburn Park. While the play was in progress, a man dressed as a chicken forced his way onto the stage and disrupted the production. The show was stopped. Stewards got the man off the stage. He was eventually found by police, smelling strongly of drink and standing in a pond.

There was a fancy dress ball at Woburn that night, and the man told officers he had been intending to go there. 'When officers saw him he tried to make out he was a bird with his arms flapping about,' an inspector told magistrates.

While the case was being heard in court, people on the public benches began to laugh. They were sternly rebuked by the magistrate, who told them, 'This is no laughing matter.'

Wayward attenders of fancy dress balls have provided the press with much colourful copy over the years. In Hendon in 1978, for example, a man dressed as a gorilla was arrested for being drunk and disorderly. He later demonstrated his gorilla act in the dock by jumping up and down and scratching his armpits, and informed magistrates that he would pay his fine in bananas.

A more significant case in the history of British law occurred at Birmingham in 1981. A building company had dismissed a man who came to work wearing a succession of eccentric and undignified hats. The case was brought before an industrial tribunal which heard that the man had been fired after he arrived wearing a trilby hat with a replica of Kermit the Frog on top.

The tribunal ruled that under the circumstances, wearing a Kermit hat was not a good reason for dismissal.

Present-day feminists maintain that there is something essentially weird about all beauty contests. Weirdest of all, however, were surely the Miss Gas Mask events organized at various seaside towns during World War Two. In our own age of permissiveness, total nudity has lost much of its power to startle. In 1935, however, a bashful girl refused to play the part of Lady Godiva at a Jubilee Pageant in Brighton. A last-minute effort was made by the organizers to find a girl willing to take the part. 'Otherwise,' reported the *Daily Telegraph*, 'the white horse will be ridden by a man wearing flesh-coloured tights and a wig of flowing golden hair.'

Even among newspaper editors themselves, a tendency towards eccentricity may sometimes be detected. A furious quarrel once erupted between the chiefs of two local papers in the United States. The editor of the *Ossego Press* wrote: 'J.T.G. Roe, editor of the Anoca *Beacon*, should be lynched, parboiled, vitriolized, quartered and his remains hung to dry on a fence. In flaming headlines he accuses us of attempted suicide in his last issue of his 2×4 measly, mangy sheet.

'This long, lean, lanky, lantern-jawed, lop-eared, lop-sided, long-faced, hollow-eyed, pot-bellied, carping, whimpering wampus, this cross between a jellyfish and a cur will answer to us, not in a libel suit, but personally.

'We admit that we were ill last Wednesday evening. But to accuse us of self-destruction could only originate in the mind of an imbecile.

'We have always safeguarded our health. It has been our custom after a hard day's work to step to the kitchen cabinet and take a tonic before retiring, and upon arising in the morning.

'We were about to retire and from custom reached into the cabinet and took a large, healthy swig and after quite a draught we noticed that the taste was off. Our better half had been housecleaning and accidentally placed a bottle of O'Cedar Cleansing Compound in the cabinet. This is what we got hold of, but we wish to say that we were only slightly indisposed for a short interval.'

The fued between American professors Alan Sandage and Halton Arp was waged in less conspicuous, but no less bitter fashion. It was learned in 1977 that for ten years the two men had occupied offices in the same corridor of the California Institute of Technology. In all that time they refused to exchange a single word. The cause of contention? They disagreed about the distance from the earth of certain objects in the universe.

Private eye David Lewis was even more persevering once he got his teeth into his subject. But in his case, the obsession was a crossword puzzle. On 23 April

---

Dummy

What nonsense to suggest, as your woman's page did last week, that the use of a dummy is either unhygienic or a bad habit which could become hard for a baby to break. I have derived great comfort from my dummy for 40 years, and find it gives much greater oral satisfaction than the unhealthy cigarette. It is also much cheaper.
Letter in *Brighton and Hove Herald*

DISORDERLY CONDUCT

The World's Weirdest War
In June 1969, the Central American football teams of Honduras and El Salvador played a series of qualifying matches for the World Cup. The games were closely fought, and El Salvador eventually won after being awarded a disputed penalty. Rioting broke out at the ground, and the fighting spilled into the streets. In July, war was declared between the two countries as a direct result of the disputed penalty. Two thousand people died in the fighting. In the next round of the World Cup, the El Salvador team was eliminated.

1933, he sat down with that week's £2,000 *News of the World* crossword puzzle. In August of 1982, he finally sent in his solution – almost 50 years after he had first embarked on it. 'Sorry I'm late, the clues rather baffled me,' he wrote, adding: 'By the time I finished the crossword I could hardly recognize the handwriting I had when I started.'

In spite of his marathon effort, however, the 67-year-old Cardiff man had got a few of the answers wrong.

In September 1982, a new by-law was passed by local authorities in an Oregon town. It decreed that at least one joke had to be told at every meeting of the town council.

What scenes of relentless tedium must have prompted this desperate act of legislation? Even the authorities are human, and in moments of whimsical inspiration have let their fancies free. The possession of marijuana plants in Mason County, Washington State, carried a maximum five years' jail sentence when a 24-year-old lorry driver was arrested in 1978 for growing them. But the offender was let off with a milder sentence. The judge ordered him instead to wheel one of his plants in a wheelbarrow full of manure 20 times round the courthouse on four successive Sundays. 'A little humility never hurt anyone,' said the judge.

In Philadelphia, a man who had stolen a chewing gum vending machine containing 250 pieces was once sentenced by a judge to chew every tab of gum in the machine. He was required to drop a penny in the slot for every piece taken out. The task completed, he had to go and give the machine, with the pennies in it, back to its owner.

A more worthwhile activity was devised by a Miami judge in June 1982. Learning that the South Florida blood service was in constant need of donars, he gave minor offenders the choice of either paying a fine or giving a pint of their own blood.

Concern for public well-being was also what prompted the sewage chief of an

All Dressed Up

Some people have made a profession out of their skill in dressing up. The *Strand Magazine* of 1894 contains an interesting account of pantomime artist Mr Charles Lauri's varied impersonations of parrots, poodles and other creatures. It also recounts a 'capital story' of how Mr Lauri was great friends with an old monkey at the London Zoo. The monkey's name was Sally, and the performer would study and imitate her movements for hours.

One sad day, Sally died. Her keepers regretted that they did not have a photograph of her. Mr Lauri told them he had plenty. He then went off, had himself made up to look like the deceased creature, and faced the camera.

Mr Lauri assured the *Strand*: 'Those keepers who have the photo I gave them believe it is Sally to this day, so far as I know.'

A capital story indeed. Unfortunately, the photographs accompanying the article make it appear deeply improbable.

American town to place the following notice in the pages of the *Flemington Democrat*:

'From time to time I have issued various warnings to the citizens of our town regarding the nature of material that comes down through our sewers. Parts of clothing, hair, gauze, muslin etc., are constantly coming through . . . And within the last six months two little boy babies have come through. Surely the time has come for a halt, or we suffer from a stoppage and probably a new sewer plant for the taxpayers.'

Theodore Bellis
Superintendent

The Voice of Authority

In England, the worthy bobby on the beat has long been among the most reassuring figures of authority. What sinister motive, then, had PC Keith Tallett, in taking down two statements in two different styles of handwriting, asked magistrates at a Nuneaton court? They were quickly reassured. The officer was 6 ft 5 in tall. It was stated that his writing sloped in different directions according to which leg he was bending.

The historic authority of the British peerage, however, must have taken a serious knock when readers of the *Daily Telegraph* discovered in 1936 that: 'Peeresses who take chocolate to the Abbey will place it in their inverted coronets. At the last Coronation they used them as sandwich holders.'

In January 1978, moreover, a question mark loomed over Buckingham Palace itself. At Portsmouth, it was announced that a special request had been issued from the palace for the great Spithead naval review. A momentous decision had been taken to change the sailors' cheer, as the Queen went by, from 'hurrah' to 'hooray'. Admiral Sir Henry Leach, Commander-in-Chief of the Fleet, said: 'I am delighted. I have felt that way all my life.'

One cannot help sympathizing with the man who tried to set fire to the British consulate in Venice in August of 1982. He did so, he said, 'because the English get on my nerves'.

Love, Marriage and Family Life

In 1981, a New Jersey man was indicted for biting the nose off his daughter's boyfriend. Not long afterwards, a 15-year-old Italian girl in Albenga was admitted to hospital seeking treatment for a dislocated jaw; she told doctors that the injury was caused by passionate kisses (her boyfriend was unhurt).

The perils of passion were illustrated in August 1982, when doctors warned that love bites which break on the skin can be fatal; only bites from rabid animals were more serious. New York doctors reported hospitals overflowing with patients bitten on ears, noses, hands, nipples and genitals. In some cases, infections had led to septic shock and death. Special dangers were reported from injuries which did not even look like bites 'because some people have incomplete dentures'.

How close the bonds uniting love and pain: 'Miss O'Neil said Wardlow picked up an axe and struck her twice on the head with it,' reported the *Edinburgh Evening News*, describing one scene of domestic discord. 'She was in bed at the time. Shortly afterwards, he hit her on the head with a can of soup. "He opened it then, and we both had the soup."'

What, after all, is love? In September 1977, psychologists and others met in Swansea for the first-ever conference on the subject which has mystified poets since the dawn of time. Their conclusion? Love is 'the cognitive-affective state characterized by intrusive or obsessive fantasizing concerning reciprocity of amorant and feeling by the object of the amorance'.

The bonds of family amorance were strained in an incident reported by the *American Mercury* which announced:

'Mrs Fred Funkey is near death from a shotgun wound, her son, Fred Funkey Jr., 22, is in a critical condition from knifewounds, and her husband, 65, is badly cut over the face and hands and is under arrest as a result of a free-for-all family fight Wednesday at their home near Arroll, in which a daughter, Lola, 17, also engaged.

'The argument is said to have started in a disagreement as to where the family should spend a holiday. The mother and children wanted to go up the creek for a picnic and the father wanted to go down the creek. Funkey is alleged to have shot his wife in the back with a shotgun loaded with two ball bearings. Funkey was then attacked by his son, who was wounded by a large knife cut which severed one rib. Coming to her brother's rescue, Lola beat the father off with a heavy plank.'

DISORDERLY CONDUCT

Up the creek? The American love of violence is celebrated worldwide, and newspaper readers will have been less startled by the following headline of August 1982, when they discovered that the incident occurred in Colorado Springs, Colorado: 'Bride's Mother Kills Groom at Reception'. The groom was indeed shot dead with a rifle bullet during a blazing row which erupted only six hours after the wedding ceremony. But the headline was slightly misleading. The mother-in-law hit the groom by accident; she was really aiming at her husband.

A more mellow mother-in-law report was issued from Colorado in the same summer, concerning the marriage of John and Paula Morris. Paula was a highly successful announcer with a local radio station. She had married John only on the understanding that they should not start a family until her career was entirely secure. So when their unplanned baby son Jason was born only a year later, Paula grew concerned about her future.

To solve the problem, John Morris gave up his job as a ski instructor and agreed to look after the child. If he needed any assistance, Paula's widowed mother, Paulette Jamieson, who lived nearby, was at hand.

The arrangement worked well enough for two years, but collapsed one evening in 1982 when Paula arrived home after a long stint at the radio station and John informed her: 'I'm suing for divorce.'

He added: 'You have become a disinterested mother and wife because of your career. Your mother and I are in love. We want to marry and also take custody of little Jason.'

Paula moved out of the house that night, and soon afterwards counter-sued for divorce, accusing her mother of adultery and also bringing a case against her mother for alienation of affections. Forty-four-year-old Mrs Jamieson, a striking blonde, told reporters: 'I don't suppose my daughter will speak to me ever again. I'm deeply sorry about that. But she has her career to think of. I have little Jason to consider.'

The divorce case was one of the most complex heard in Colorado. In contrast, a very rapid conclusion was reached at Jacksonville, Florida, in December 1972. Rudell Hickson and his wife, Mary, were in a divorce court trying to be separated. Instead, they got into an argument, both pulled guns and blazed away at each other from opposite ends of a conference table in the judge's hearing room. Bullets flew in all directions.

A police officer was giving testimony in an adjoining courtroom when the gun battle broke out. He borrowed a pistol from a circuit judge, chased Mrs Hickson down the hall and ordered her to halt. When she failed to do so, he shot the unfortunate woman dead.

Sometimes, of course, one partner in a marriage may refuse to grant the divorce desired by the other. Many and various are the solutions to which frustrated individuals have resorted. Thomas Karkanias, for example, a bus conductor from central Greece, was charged with rigging up the kitchen cooker to murder his wife by electrocution. A South African woman in Johannesburg's wealthy white suburbs was charged with trying to poison her husband by treating his hamburger with swimming pool chemicals.

In general, however, jealous love must surely be the most common motive for crimes of violence. The love triangle has provided the theme for countless works of pulp fiction as well as for some of the world's greatest works of literature. The torments known to Othello were known to Mr Graham Street, of Dudley in Worcestershire:

'Springheeled Husband Pounced on Lovers' announced the *Daily Telegraph* of 6 December 1974. The irate Mr Street flew into action on a homemade catapult when he saw his wife being cuddled by another man. He made a springboard out of a long plank and two car tyres, and after a long run-up launched himself into the air. Propelled at high speed, Mr Street crashed head-first through the kitchen window of the house where his wife was enjoying the embraces of another man. The human cannonball landed in the sink and slid gently to the floor.

Graham Street pleaded guilty to causing £1.49 damage to the window and was told by the judge not to indulge in such 'amateur dramatics' again.

If the springheeled husband's motive was jealousy, what caused Mrs Hughes of Preston in Lancashire to stab her husband 15 times with a kitchen knife as he lay peacefully in his sleep? Not even Mrs Hughes could provide a satisfactory answer; she was as bewildered by her actions as everyone else.

The case was reported in May 1978, and made strange reading. Linda Hughes was brought for trial accused of wounding her husband Frank with intent to cause grievous bodily harm. The court heard how Mr Hughes was taken to hospital with collapsed lungs after his wife's savage assault. But Mrs Hughes herself was asleep at the time. She was freed when the prosecution dropped the charges, admitting that: 'According to psychiatric opinion it is certainly feasible that what she did she did in her sleep.' The judge agreed that no purpose would be served by a trial.

'I just cannot explain what happened,' Mrs Hughes told reporters. 'Apparently I am what is called a disturbed sleeper. But there is no other reason for it. I was half asleep when I got up to peel some potatoes for the next day. I must have had the knife from then.' The couple had been happily married for ten years and had two children. The moaning husband managed to awaken his spouse during the course of the attack. She said, 'You can imagine what an awful shock it was when I saw what was happening. I telephoned for an ambulance straight away.'

Mrs Hughes left the court arm-in-arm with her husband.

Curious Crime

The title of Britain's Most Optimistic Burglar was awarded by the *Sunday Times* to a Yorkshireman with a withered hand, an artificial leg and one eye missing who was advised by magistrates to take up 'a more rewarding occupation' after his seventh conviction, in March 1977.

Thieves come in all shapes and sizes, and people will steal practically anything. In August 1982, for example, *The Times* reported from Washington that: 'The Smithsonian Institution has found the bottom half of George Washington's stolen dentures but the FBI is still hunting the uppers.'

Obsessive would-be doctors and dentists are a recognized type of criminal impostor. In March 1981, a particularly bizarre case was reported. A hospital filing clerk had become so obsessed with surgery that he built a secret operating theatre in an attic. He fitted it out with £3,000 worth of medical equipment stolen from the Warwick hospital in which he worked. There were scalpels, clamps, oxygen cylinders, trolleys, chemicals and hundreds of other surgical accessories. In this weird Aladdin's Cave of appliances, the man carried out experiments on rats and rabbits. He was caught when a porter at the hospital saw him loading an anaesthetic trolley into a car.

The Trouser Thief of Toronto was apprehended in 1938. For 33 years he had stolen nothing but trousers. 'His record goes back to 1905,' said the prosecutor, 'and only once, in 1907, did he lapse from his standard and steal anything but a pair of trousers. On that occasion it was a shirt.'

The Trouser Thief was a specialist. So too was Peter Kelly, 'a most horrible annoyance', whose arrest was reported in *The Times* of 12 October 1837. The report is worth quoting verbatim for it shows that however times and crimes may change, the newspapers' interest in off-beat episodes has remained unaltered over the years:

'Peter Kelly, a pauper of St Sepulchre's parish church, was charged with having undressed himself for the purpose of exciting the charitable feeling of the public more effectually.

'A constable stated, that to his great astonishment he saw the prisoner go up stark naked (with the exception of the abdomen, round which was tied a piece of old rag) to a hall in Finsbury Circus and knock boldly. The females all ran away the moment they beheld such an object, for he was not only destitute of clothing, but he had not shaved for six months. Upon being repulsed at one door, the prisoner went up to another, and the witness learned that he asked for charity wherever he knocked.

'Mr Miller, one of the parish officers, said, that the prisoner had been a pauper all his life, and had been in every prison within 50 miles of London. The plan he adopted of going naked was very ingenious, and sure to tell among the humane, who would drop a few pence and run away.

The Lord Mayor – He looks like an idiot.

Mr Miller – he is about a quarter of a fool and three quarters of a knave, and he is the most horrible annoyance, for when he fancies getting money, he tears his clothes off and knocks loudly at the doors of the most respectable houses. When we catch him at such tricks we generally put him in a sack, with his head through one hole and his legs through two others.'

Kelly's defence, incidentally, was that he considered it quite warm enough to go about the streets with no clothes on. In modern days, he might have made a passably good insurance swindler. Certainly he could have fared no worse than the motorcyclist whose case came up in September 1982. He tried to swindle £100,000 out of an insurance company by getting his girlfriend to chop off his foot. Phase One of the master plan was successful – the foot came off. Phase Two was less so – nobody was fooled. The man was jailed in San José, California.

Reflecting on his misfortunes, the footloose defrauder might do well to consider a career as a drug smuggler. Or perhaps not. One 46-year-old thought he would be free from suspicion because of his physical handicap. But when he stepped of a plane from Caracas, Venezuela, he was arrested by narcotics agents in New York.

The agents came up empty-handed when they searched his luggage. Then, noticing his wooden leg, they took him to the nearest hospital and removed it in the presence of a doctor. Hidden in a compartment in the leg, neatly encased in a plastic bag, was 18 ounces of cocaine, worth $65,000.

The man pleaded guilty to drug possession and was sentenced to four years in prison. While serving his term, the smuggler made an appeal against the validity of the search, claiming that federal agents had violated his right to

---

The World's Most Determined Murderess

This title belongs to a 36-year-old American woman who devised a series of bizarre schemes to murder her husband, finally succeeding at San Diego, California. The case was reported in January 1978.

She put LSD in his toast, served him blackberry pie containing the venom sac of a tarantula spider, placed bullets in the carburettor of his lorry, tossed a live electric wire into his shower, and injected air into his veins with a hypodermic needle to induce a heart attack.

She finally succeeded by dropping tranquillizers into his beer and smashing his skull with a steel weight.

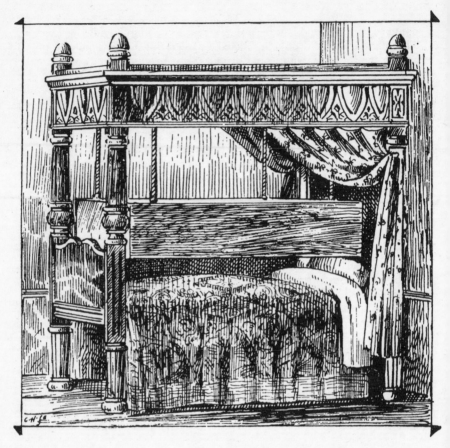

Nightmare device – the suffocating bedstead

privacy. The appeal was launched with a cheerful optimism and it was turned down.

A 45-year-old Düsseldorf man lodged no such appeal, but then his plan had been twice as ambitious. In 1978, in Bangkok, he was jailed for five years for trying to smuggle about 2 lb of morphine out of Thailand in his two artificial legs.

Criminal ingenuity knows no bounds. The *Strand Magazine* of 1894 illustrates a suffocating bedstead devised by the landlord of a wayside coaching inn. It comprised a massive wooden box which was lowered over sleeping travellers to imprison them in an air-tight cavity. Their possessions could then be stolen without risk, and the bodies disposed of afterwards. The means by which a Brooklyn housewife was killed in May 1982 was equally macabre. A package arrived at her home, and when she opened it in her kitchen she found a volume entitled *Quick and Delicious Gourmet Cookbook*. She lifted the cover. Immediately, there was a blinding flash and two .22-calibre bullets tore into her chest; she died three hours later. 'It took a lot of thinking to make that bomb,' an inspector later commented. The cookbook was only $1\frac{1}{2}$ in thick, but it had been hollowed out to enclose a six-volt battery wired to a charge of gunpowder and three bullets. At the time of writing, neither motive nor murderer were known for sure.

How unfeeling the modern criminal can be! In September 1982, the *Daily Mirror* reported: 'A group called the Pixie Eradication Society has been smashing garden gnomes on Dartmoor "to rid the national park of these distasteful little objects".'

The action of a Philadelphia banker was more curious still. He shook hands with a Philadelphia woman after church service. The alleged atrocity was committed in 1975. Two years later, the woman claimed, her hand still hurt and she brought a suit against the banker for $10,000 damages. Her husband launched a related suit on his own behalf, seeking $10,000 for himself because he had been 'deprived of his wife's assistance in society'; the case of the Golden Handshake?

The banker was accused of negligence in 'pulling, squeezing and shaking the woman's hand' without considering the strength and power of his hand grip. The case of two senior citizens of Cleveland, Ohio, provides a finale for this chapter on crime. The men must be classed as the World's Worst Gunslingers. After the event, which occurred in 1981, they were released having signed papers saying that they did not wish to press charges against one another and their names were not released. One, however, was aged 77 and the other 76.

The men had a grudge that went back a long way. They lived in flats opposite one another and began quarrelling, as they had often done before, in the narrow hallway of an apartment house one Tuesday morning. On this occasion, however, mere insults could not quench their rage. Each went back to his apartment block and returned brandishing a venerable six-shooter. Then they began to blaze away.

Both shot their full load – 12 bullets were fired in all – and alarmed residents called the police. 'There were bullet holes above, bullet holes down, and bullet holes all over the hallway,' said a detective. But every one had gone astray. Police suggested that the gunslingers missed because one needed a cane to prop himself up and the other had trouble seeing because of a glaucoma. They were standing just five feet apart during the duel.

Domestic Lock-Ups

An irreverent rhyme, much loved by schoolchildren, runs:

> *Oh dear, what can the matter be?*
> *Three old ladies locked in the lavatory*
> *They were there from Monday to Saturday*
> *Nobody knew they were there*

Fact almost imitated fiction in August 1982, when two elderly French ladies suffered an even longer period of incarceration. A widow of 94 and her 66-year-old daughter spent nine days locked in a lavatory at their Paris flat. They had been forced inside the toilet by a burglar who jammed two armchairs against the door before fleeing the scene. Their cries were not heard, and they survived on water from the wash basin until a worried relative contacted the police.

From the outside, the incident may have appeard to have its humorous aspects; from the inside, there can have been little to laugh at. Another story broke in France in the same month, and about this case there was absolutely nothing amusing whatsoever. On 23 August the newspapers announced that a 12-year-old French boy had been kept locked up in a cupboard at his home for seven full years.

The ordeal of young David Brisson was revealed by the public prosecutor at Evry, in the southern suburbs of Paris. David had been found asleep in a garden one morning during the previous week. He explained to police that he had escaped from his home in a nearby block of flats. He could not read or write and had never been to school. The boy was less than four feet tall and weighed only four-and-a-half stone.

The police discovered that David was the son of Françoise Brisson, a 36-year-old cashier. Her marriage had broken up soon after the boy was born and he was sent to foster parents. Françoise began to live with a supermarket manager named Claude Chevet. They had a son of their own, and the child of the earlier marriage became the subject of inhuman neglect.

When David was five his mother brought him to live with her new family. There was no warm welcome. She and Chevet locked him in a cupboard and gave him nothing but bread and water. For the last two years of his ordeal, the boy lived under a shelf unit, in a floor space of five feet by two feet, with no light.

In February 1982 the rest of the family went away for a winter sports holiday, leaving David nothing but some fruit, dry biscuits and water to keep him alive for eight days. When they returned, the familiar pattern resumed again. Then, for once, Françoise forgot to lock the cupboard and David escaped. It was the parents' turn to know the distress of incarceration as they awaited trial.

It has been said by some ardent feminists that being a housewife is in itself a form of imprisonment. An Italian mother, Elena Pau, however, was not one of these. Signora Pau was sentenced by a courts for selling furniture placed under sequestration by the court, after pleading that she had done it to buy food for her seven children (she lived with them and her husband in two rooms). Almost immediately, however, the woman became pregnant, and under Italian law a woman could not be imprisoned in that condition for six months after the birth. When the allotted time was up, Signora Pau triumphantly presented a second medical certificate – she was pregnant again. The protection provided by the birth of her ninth child ended on 17 May 1973. But when the police went to arrest her they found that she had already provided herself with a new certificate – to say that her tenth child was on the way.

Panic in the Streets

In March 1957, villagers at Wardle near Rochdale saw a sinister, glowing object hovering ominously over their small community. From it emanated an eerie white light. So great was local concern about the UFO that questions were even asked in Parliament about it. Were the aliens poised for invasion?

The answer came in the House of Commons, when the Air Minister was questioned about the Rochdale Thing. Amid laughter, an under-secretary replied: 'This object, which was described in the Press as a flying saucer, did not emanate from outer space, but from a laundry in Rochdale. It consisted of two hydrogen-filled balloons illuminated by a flashlight bulb and devised by a laundry mechanic.'

Questioned by reporters, the mechanic revealed himself to be an amateur meteorologist who had created the device as an experiment in tracing air currents.

The case is just one among many UFO 'flaps'. On New Year's Eve in 1978, for example, television viewers throughout Europe were riveted by the screening of some mysterious objects filmed over New Zealand. At the same time, a cigar-shaped craft with flaming portholes was widely reported in Europe itself. A Cheshire surgeon and his neighbour, a builder, were among the first to spot the object. 'It was cigar-shaped with a broad, trailing vapour jet,' said the surgeon. 'It moved in a straight line with no noise. I have always been sceptical about these things, but this defied any orthodox analysis.' His neighbour confirmed the description: he saw 'portholes aflame with incandescence'.

Though some controversy still lingers around the New Zealand sightings, the cigar-shaped craft proved easier to explain. It was the burning debris of a Soviet rocket which had launched the satellite Cosmos 1068 into space, and which crashed in West Germany.

Unquestionably the most famous flap, however, occurred in the New York area in late October 1938 – before the term 'flying saucer' had even been coined. *The Times* reported: 'All began after 8 o'clock last night, when a dramatization of Mr H.G. Wells's fantasy *The War of the Worlds* came on the air over the national network of the Columbia broadcasting system. The programme was the work of Mr Orson Welles, a young American who is known as an innovator on the New York stage. He dramatizes a book or play every Sunday night on the wireless.'

In Orson Welles's ingenious production, the story was presented in a contemporary American setting. A weather report was given in a deadpan voice, followed by a programme of dance music from a fictional hotel. In the middle of a number, a newsflash was delivered concerning a gas explosion on Mars. Further news bulletins and descriptions followed: A meteor had landed near Princeton, New Jersey, killing 1,500 people. No, it wasn't a meteor, it was a metal cylinder. The top unscrewed – monsters crawled out armed with death rays – bullets could not stop them – they were marching on New York – martial law had been declared and the state militia were out.

The Martians were coming! At least they were as far as hundreds of panic-stricken listeners were concerned. Telephone lines to police stations were soon jammed. People rushed into the streets, many of them with towels over their faces as gas masks. Less excitable souls telephoned the authorities offering to help in the emergency. Even church services were interrupted.

Three times during the programme it was explained that the events were only part of a radio programme, but these announcements failed to stop the panic. Eventually, a series of reassuring pronouncements from Columbia officials, police and news services did manage to restore peace. Columbia, however, faced heavy criticism in the ensuing days – though the publicity did Orson Welles's career no harm.

UFO flaps have generally resulted from honest mistakes, and have seldom caused long-term distress. A very different kind of panic gripped the small French village of Pont-Saint-Esprit in August 1951. It was as if a collective hysteria of mediaeval intensity had been visited upon the community.

Contemporary English language newspapers dealt only briefly with the story, but a full account is given in *The Day of St. Anthony's Fire* by John G. Fuller

(Hutchinson, 1969). I have drawn on the book for much of the material below.

Hundreds of inhabitants felt the symptoms: giddiness, diarrhoea, vomiting and other effects. But for many the experience was much more alarming. Five-year-old Marie-Joseph Carle, for example, saw blood dripping from her bedroom ceiling; there were tigers by the wall and they were coming to eat her. Her father found himself endlessly counting the six panes on his window, day and night; flies were everywhere and he craved bead curtains for them to rest on. A young engineer could think of nothing but potatoes. A certain M. Delacquis saw exploding flowers, and knew the secrets of the universe.

It grew worse. Lying in his bedroom, M. Sauvet became a circus performer, a strong man whose pillow cases turned to iron bars which he ripped to shreds effortlessly. Giant timbers splintered in his hands while an invisible audience of admirers cheered deliriously – his bedstead was ruined. The hallucinations were interspersed with bouts of exhausted lethargy when the unfortunate man knew who he was, and lay in dread of the next convulsive fantasy. One night the awful elation came with special force. His night-clothes became tight-fitting leotards. He strutted from his bedroom and into the streets, reaching a temporary suspension bridge above the Rhône, where for fifteen minutes he performed a tightrope act high above the watching villagers. He was rescued, jerking and trembling on a cable, by two gendarmes.

Joseph Puche thought he was an aeroplane. He leapt from a second storey window shouting 'I can fly! Don't all of you believe me? Watch!' He shattered both of his legs. Bleeding severely, he rose on two broken legs and ran fifty metres down a boulevard before they caught him; it took eight men and two doctors to get him to hospital.

The hospital itself was overflowing with victims of delusion, shrieking and moaning night after night. One man was being chased by bandits with huge donkey ears. Another was tormented by writhing red snakes in his brain. One woman spat fire from her fingers; another thought she was a baroness and deserved better treatment than she was getting.

There were only three strait-jackets in the hospital, and though the place was ringed by police and firemen, moaning patients were constantly breaking loose and carrying their horrors back into the streets.

And the cause of this appalling visitation? A batch of loaves made by a village baker had been affected by ergot fungus, a mould which forms on certain grains and which causes psychic disturbance (LSD is an ergot alkaloid). Ergotism had been thought a thing of the past. In the Middle Ages, whole villages had sometimes been afflicted with a terrifying collective madness which was known as St Anthony's fire; the episode at Pont-Saint-Esprit was a freak recurrence of the ancient malady. Five people died, and of the 300 or so affected by the 'accursed bread' there were many who never truly recovered from their ordeal

Chapter Three

Loners

The bizarre behaviour of certain individuals has given them a kind of grotesque grandeur. Such was the case with two Japanese soldiers who continued to fight World War Two, decades after the conflict was over. Such was also the case with Dr Mary Walker, the top-hatted and much persecuted pioneer of rational dress in America. The affair of the Buckingham Palace Intruder obsessed the British press in 1982, while the no-less sensational case of Colonel Barker exploded like a bombshell in the newspapers of 1929.

The Case of Colonel Barker

Early in 1927, Captain Leslie Ivor Victor Gauntlett Bligh Barker, DSO, a former cavalry officer, had a brush with the London police. Captain Barker was a prominent member of the National Fascisti movement in London. Police had raided its headquarters, where the captain was found to be in possession of a pistol with a forged firearms certificate.

The case received little attention in the press. The Captain was prosecuted at the Central Criminal Court for submitting a forged document with intention to deceive. Captain Barker made his way into the courtroom with his eyes bandaged, and was led into the dock by a friend. It was explained that the defendant suffered from bouts of blindness owing to wounds incurred during the Great War. There was some sympathy for the ex-officer, with his distinguished service record. He was acquitted of the charge on the grounds that the certificate was not a public document.

Captain Barker was a popular figure in the National Fascisti movement, which was disbanded shortly after the court case. He also ran a restaurant in the West End, and it was when this venture foundered, and Barker failed to appear in a bankruptcy court, that the sensational story broke.

In March 1929, Colonel Barker, as he now styled himself, was arrested and taken to Brixton prison. When a routine medical examination was proposed, Colonel Barker objected. He could not submit to it, he said, because he was a woman.

The doctors examined the accused, and confirmed his story. The colonel was immediately taken to the women's prison at Holloway.

Who was 'he'? How had 'he' got away with 'his' masquerade for so long? What were 'his' motives? The press reports which followed were spangled with apostrophes referring to 'him' and 'his' exploits. For ease of reading, we will dispense with the inverted commas and refer to Colonel Barker as a he, as a tribute to his amazing imposture. But a woman he certainly was.

When the astounding discovery was made, the newspapers scrambled for interviews with those who had known him. Old Fascisti members were nonplussed. Barker had hunted and boxed with them, and seemed a 'jolly good fellow'. *Evening Standard* reporters contacted J. Moss Ltd, a firm of military outfitters, whose bemused staff produced correspondence from the colonel recording their dealings with him. Only recently, Barker had come in for a new uniform, explaining that he had been promoted to staff colonel at the War

Colonel Barker – "a jolly good fellow" according to friends

Office: 'He was always dressed well. His thick dark hair was always brushed well back from the forehead.'

A number of people around Cambridge Circus knew him as the 'DSO Colonel'. He had claimed to be one of the Old Contemptibles and wore the Mons Star of the veterans' association. 'Sometimes he would hint that he was in the Secret Service,' said an acquaintance.

A former landlady said: 'I think it was wonderful that he was able to keep up the pretence of a man. If I saw him again I should shake him by the hand.'

But the most remarkable fact to emerge during the first interviews was that Colonel Barker had a wife and children.

The whole bizarre story unfolded over several weeks, first, as the press tracked down the wife, and later, as the Colonel himself was prosecuted in court for obtaining a marriage licence by deceit.

Colonel Barker's maiden name was Lillias Irma Valerie Barker. Legally, she was Mrs Arkell-Smith. The daughter of a William Barker, she was born on 26 August 1895, in Jersey. In 1912 she was sent to a convent in Brussels, and when war broke out she served as a VAD nurse in a Surrey hospital. Later she was employed at an army remount depot.

In April 1918 she married Lieutenant Harold Arkell-Smith, an Australian. It was only six months, however, before they separated. After the war she helped to run a tea-shop in Warminster, and while there she met another Australian soldier named Pearce-Crouch. Her life of deception began with a modest masquerade. The couple started living together as man and wife; and by Pearce-Crouch she bore two children, a boy and a girl.

Pearce-Crouch was a violent man, and the relationship appears to have been stormy. While passing as the Australian's wife, Barker took to wearing the masculine attire of the Land Girl – riding breeches, open-necked coat and shirt. And dressed in this fashion, she started to develop a liaison with Alfreda Haward, the daughter of a local chemist at Littlehampton.

She told the girl that she was really a man, and her name was Sir Victor Barker, a baronet. They began to go courting. Barker explained that his father was dead, and that his mother had forced him to wear women's clothing. Miss Haward apparently swallowed the story, and after a violent fight between Barker and Pearce-Crouch, the lovers eloped. On 14 November 1923, Sir Victor Barker and Miss Alfreda Haward were married at a Brighton church.

Was Miss Haward really deceived? By her own account she certainly was. It would be distasteful to speculate at length on what passed during the honeymoon. Barker told the girl that during the war he had received 'serious abdominal wounds'.

'I know it seems incredible that I could have been deceived as I was,' Miss Haward told *Evening Standard* reporters, 'but not once during the three years we

The Human Mole

In 1974, father-of-six Norman Green was questioned by police about a rape case. Although he had nothing to do with it, he was frightened of being wrongly convicted and went into hiding. As the months went by, his disappearance was accepted in the neighbourhood.

Eight years passed. His six children grew up at their home in Ince, Wigan, without the benefit of Mr Green's fatherly guidance. But his wife, Pauline, made do as best she could, winning much sympathy from the neighbours.

And then, in July 1982, Norman Green came out of hiding. He was pale and emaciated from his long ordeal – for during the entire period when he was believed missing, Mr Green had been hiding under the floorboards of his own home.

Only his wife had known of his whereabouts; she had taken him meals and tried to keep his spirits up. The children had been completely ignorant of their father's hiding place. And when Mr Green finally emerged to face questioning on the rape case he was told that the police had ruled him out long since – they were not looking for him at all.

lived together did I suspect that my husband was anything but what he pretended to be – a war injured officer.' She did, however, doubt his claims to be a baronet:

'I said it would be much better for both of us if he forgot the title. Frankly, I thought it was a little bit of conceit on his part, and assumed that he might have some distant claim to the title.

'Our life was fairly happy until towards the end of 1926, when I had to go into a nursing home to be operated on for appendicitis. After the operation I went down to Littlehampton to stay with my people until I recuperated. In January 1927 I received a letter from him saying that he had decided to finish with me and could not live with me again. It was a terrible blow to me, but I decided that I could nothing but stay at home. I could not appeal to him. I was much too proud to do that.

'I know that some members of my own family were not keen on the marriage, particularly because my father could not find any reference to 'Sir Victor Barker' in our book of titles. I am afraid it was I who clinched matters by saying that I trusted Victor more than anybody in the world.'

The discovery of Colonel Barker's masquerade came to her as a 'thunderbolt'; she had first learnt of it through the newspapers.

During the *Evening Standard* interview, the girl's father said: 'My daughter is a fine, straight girl, and it is dreadful to think that she has been deceived in this way. It has ruined her life. I thought she would be happy so I gave my consent to the marriage. I have since been blamed for not making more careful inquiries, and I wish to goodness now that I had.' The girl's mother said: 'It is terrible to think that a woman could be so wicked.'

In a *Sunday Express* exclusive, Miss Haward expanded on her marriage presenting Colonel Barker as a near-ideal husband:

'I always called him Bill,' she said. 'It is such a manly name. It suited him beautifully. I do not think we got on better or worse than countless couples. I think most people would say we were happy. Our marriage was a perfectly normal one.' If her husband had a fault, it was his eye for the ladies. 'Everything was all right until another woman came onto the scene. She made him do anything she wanted. He left me with scarcely an explanation. I always knew Bill was susceptible. He could never see a pretty woman without paying her compliments and saying pretty things to her.

'I must say "he" and "him" because anything else is strange to me. I cannot believe that he is anything else. It is too fantastic. I feel as if the whole thing is a fearful nightmare from which I shall wake up. I wish I could.'

It was after leaving his wife that Barker got involved with the National Fascisti. And by a curious coincidence, the prosecutor at the trial over firearms possession was the same man who prosecuted Barer for giving a false name on his marriage licence. The Recorder at the later trial was astounded:

The Recorder – She stood trial in this court as a man?

The Prosecutor – Yes. Not a soul in court – I prosecuted her on that occasion – was aware that there was other than a man in the dock.

Barker's defending counsel stated that there was no law against a woman dressing up as a man. He cited Joan of Arc who had recently been canonized. Male clothing had been necessary to his client if she was to make a career for herself, having left Pearce-Crouch. Miss Haward's father was far from being reluctant to allow his daughter to marry the mystery baronet – it was he who had forced the couple into the ceremony. Barker did plead guilty, however, to the charge of 'knowingly and wilfully causing a false statement to be entered on a register of marriage'.

Lillias Arkell-Smith, alias 'Colonel Barker', was found guilty and sentenced to nine months imprisonment. The case had exploded like a bombshell in an age where transvestism was a subject less familiar to the general public than it is today. By any standards, however, it had been a bizarre affair, and some lenience was shown to the defendant on account of 'what she has suffered owing to the great interest which the public has taken and is taking in her when she is going through the great ordeal of her life'.

The Recorder – One might almost use the words 'prurient interest'.

Defending Counsel – Yes, My Lord.

The Rational Dresser

An article in the *Penny Pictorial Magazine* of 20 January 1900 billed her as The Most Eccentric Woman in the World, It told readers: 'Every adult in America who can read is able to answer the question, "Who is Doctor Mary Walker?".' In England, it continued, readers were less likely to be familiar with the name, unless it evoked faint memories from some stray newspaper paragraph. For the English were then not much interested in the two questions of dress reform and higher education for women, issues which were then raging in the American press.

Dr Mary Walker, who died in 1919, was an important pioneer of women's rights. If contemporary newspapermen regarded her as the World's Weirdest Woman, it was partly because her campaigns broke entirely new ground so far as the question of clothing was concerned. Dr Walker regarded tight corseting and billowing skirts as unnecessary and unhygienic fetters of womanhood. 'She has for the last forty years worn *trousers*,' explained the awestruck article in the *Pictorial Magazine*. Time and again she was arrested and imprisoned for wearing men's dress, though her record of service during the American Civil War ought to have earned her better treatment.

During the war between the North and South, she had been an assistant surgeon with the Federal forces. She was wounded in battle, and captured by the Confederates, who released her, however, when they discovered her true sex. Because of the injuries she received in the war, she sued the United States Government for a pension of four hundred pounds a year. She was, nonetheless, the only woman to be awarded a bronze star for her wartime services. It was inscribed: 'The Congress of the United States to Dr Mary E. Walker, Surgeon, U.S.A.', and Dr Walker was justly proud of the unique tribute.

It might seem that the press dealt unfairly with what was, after all, a perfectly sensible campaign. Certainly, the good doctor looked rather strange in her top hat, frock coat and cravat; but that was partly due to the absurdly fussy nature of contemporary male attire. Dr Walker called it 'rational dress'; by modern standards it was grotesquely irrational. Yet who today would complain of a woman in jeans and a T-shirt?

'A bright, dapper little woman, whose hair is turning slightly grey, and through whose gold-rimmed spectacles twinkle a pair of bright, kindly eyes, such is Dr Mary Walker, the acknowledged leader of the dress reform movement in America.' So the article described her physical appearance, also noting a round, boyish face, rather masculine features with hair cut short and parted at the side (she abhorred ringlets and curls).

The young Dr
Mary Walker –
later she
abandoned
skirts entirely

And yet, for all her commonsense and humanity, it has to be admitted that Dr Walker was something of an eccentric. For example, she founded a colony for women on a farm of 137 acres near Oswego. It was occupied only by women, bound like nuns to celibacy – but unlike nuns the occupants had to wear men's clothing. She declared herself president of the community, which was governed

---

Sign of the Chimes
Mr Peter Randall, the Town Crier at Torbay, Devon, who was
forbidden to ring his bell last week because of an old by-law, was
back in action yesterday – carrying a placard saying: 'Ding dong!'
Daily Telegraph

---

by an annually elected management board. It had its own judges and policing
system. Horses and bicycles were laid on for recreation, but there were no side-
saddles – all women were compelled to ride astride.

As for her personal vagaries, the *Pictorial Magazine* reported a typical
incident. She had recently walked into the shop of a well-known Washington
photographer who immediately recognized her as the celebrated champion of
rational dress.

'I want you to make a photograph of me in a coffin,' said Dr Mary. 'Have you
got a coffin handy in your studio? I want to see exactly how I shall look when
I'm dead.'

There was, as it happened, no coffin lying about the studio. Gamely, the
photographer suggested that she might lie in a large crate in which a new iron
bath had just arrived, and which was then lying in his back yard. He could
cover it over with curtains and muslin, he assured his customer, and no one
would know the difference. So the crate was brought in, a sofa pillow was placed
at the head, and Dr Mary solemnly stepped in. Lying down, she closed her eyes
and set her face as if in death.

The photographer carefully draped the crate with curtains, placed his
camera in position and prepared for the macabre shot. Just as he was about to
press the button, however, the death mask came alive and Dr Mary started up
exclaiming: 'Goodness, I had almost forgotten the bird. Mr Photographer, I
want the picture to show a pretty bird kissing me as I lie dead. If you haven't a
stuffed bird around here, send out and get one from the taxidermist's.'

And there she calmly lay until the photographer's assistant had gone out and
borrowed a stuffed hummingbird from a taxidermist's shop. The photo was
then taken.

It was almost twenty years before real death came to claim Dr Walker and the
indefatigable campaigner had many battles ahead. She lived to witness the rise
of the suffragette movement, the contribution that women made to efforts in
World War One, and the extension of votes to women which followed.
Obituary notices referred to her as 'the original suffragette' and before her
death she had received special dispensation from Congress granting her the
right to wear men's clothes.

Japan's Wartime Survivors

Nineteen seventy two was the year of President Nixon's historic visit to China, which opened a new era in East-West relations; it was the year in which Palestinian terrorists disrupted the Munich Olympics, and also the year of Coppola's blockbusting film, *The Godfather*. Man had long since walked on the moon, and the women's liberation movement was already a force to be reckoned with.

And yet, for a lonely recluse hiding out on the Pacific island of Guam, it was as if World War Two had never ended. On 26 January, *The Times* reported:

'A Japanese soldier who remained faithful to his orders never to surrender was captured yesterday after 28 years of hiding.

'Sergeant Shoichi Yokoi, now 56, was surprised at nightfall by two hunters in the heavily wooded Talofo River district, 20 miles from Agana, while on his way to the river to set a trap for fish. They covered him with their rifles and marched him to a police station.'

Yokoi was heavily bearded when found, wearing trousers and jacket made from tree and bark fibre. He had been a tailor when conscripted in 1941, and used a pair of scissors he had had throughout the war to shape the clothes and to cut his hair. He told reporters that he had lived since the war on a diet of nuts, breadfruit, mangoes, papya, shrimps, snails, rats and frogs. He had never heard either of the atomic bomb, or of television, and stared in disbelief when told that a jet aircraft could return him to his home town of Nagoya in three hours.

For 28 years, Sergeant Yokoi had lived in a time warp. He told reporters that he and two other Japanese fled into the jungles of Guam when American troops recaptured the island in 1944. They knew that on Guam, at least, the war was over, because of leaflets they found scattered through the jungle. But of the larger dimension, they were quite ignorant. Yokoi and his two comrades held out, fearing they might be executed if they surrendered: 'We dug a cave in a bamboo thicket but after a few months our food ran out. The others moved to a new hiding place where there was more food. We visited each other.' About eight years before his discovery, Yokoi had gone to the cave where the others were living, and found them dead. 'I believe they died of starvation,' he said. Yokoi himself had been ill several times: 'I caught a pig and apparently did not cook it very well. Another time I became numb and feared I was starving.'

Yokoi had burned his service uniform on orders. Besides his tailor's scissors, the only relics he kept from his army days were a waistband embroidered by his mother and a Japanese flag, both of which he had hidden in the cave. 'I stayed close to the cave all the time I was in the jungle,' he said. 'I never went out except at night and always stayed in the same area.' The two hunters had almost bumped into him in the dark.

Speaking of the future, he said: 'I would like to be reunited with my family and then go up a mountain and meditate for a long time.' In fact, he had only one surviving blood relative, whose wife informed reporters that the family had been told in September 1944 that Yokoi had been killed 'somewhere in the Pacific'. Before being transferred to Guam in 1943, his parents had arranged a marriage for him. Yokoi had no idea if his fiancée was even alive.

Doctors at a Guam hospital said that Yokoi's blood pressure, heart and pulse were normal, but he seemed to be anaemic as a result of his salt-free diet. Arrangements were made for his return to Japan as soon as his health permitted. 'This is like a dream to me,' said the soldier. 'I am only afraid I will wake up.'

After the initial reports, the press filled in some of the details. It appeared that Yokoi was the third former Japanese soldier to have been found on Guam long after the war was over; two others had been discovered 16 years earlier. Yokoi was entitled to back pay and allowances for his lonely years of struggle in the jungle. The sum 43.131 Yen (about £54). This pittance was calculated from the wage of nine Yen a month which he received in 1944 when he was a corporal. Nine Yen at that time was worth about 56p – about 1p in 1972. Officials considered giving Yokoi further compensation, however, and he would also be entitled to a military pension of 10.00 Yen (£12.50) a month.

Yokoi's story struck disturbing chords in the Japanese imagination, echoing largely forgotten values of samurai loyalty and discipline. In a macabre episode four Japanese boys aged from eight to ten, who tried to build a tunnelled cave like Yokoi's on Guam, were killed when the roof fell in on them. And if Japan was haunted by Yokoi's experience, so was the survivor himself. In the Guam hospital where he was being cared for, he suffered nightmares about the spirits of departed comrades, who scolded him for planning to return to Japan alone.

Yokoi slept only fitfully, crouching against a wall in a position which recalled the way he had slept in his jungle hideout. During the day he brooded, holding his head in his hands. He broke out into cold sweats and muttered that a ghost was standing at his bedside, admonishing him for having deserted his comrades. Doctors were alarmed about his mental condition. A Japanese journalist reported: 'He seems to be making a desperate effort to find an exit from the "time tunnel" that separates his former world from today's civilization.'

Guam itself had now become a popular resort for Japanese tourists. When Yokoi saw honeymooning couples, the men with long hair, the girls in hot pants, he stared in disbelief: 'Are they really Japanese?' he asked. The reporters

LONERS

themselves were an enigma to him. 'You are different Japanese,' he said. 'There must be other Japanese people.'

Eventually, the doctors considered him fit enough to leave the hospital and return to Japan. He was brought back on an aircraft which also bore home the ashes of his two comrades, who had died of starvation. Yokoi's return was a nationally televised event, which aroused intense curiosity.

About 5,000 people gathered at the airport. Among them were many veterans of the old Imperial Army. One, dressed in his former uniform, held up a banner declaring: 'Only Mr Yokoi still possesses the Spirit of Japan.' An official reception, headed by the Welfare Minister, was at hand. Yokoi emerged unsteadily from the aircraft, supported by medical attendants and waving a pink handtowel to acknowledge flagwaving and cries of 'Banzai' from the crowd. On arrival, the remains of his comrades, contained in white boxes, were presented to weeping relatives.

At a crowded press conference held later, Yokoi looked tired and drawn but surprisingly fit. Questions had been carefully prepared by Japanese journalists, inviting the former soldier to express joy on returning and to make suitably appropriate comments about the horrors of war. To their embarrassment, Yokoi appeared not to share the expected sentiments. He was ashamed to come back, he said, and his sole purpose was to give a full report on what happened at Guam as this might be useful if Japan had to fight another war.

Yokoi spoke in dry, staccato sentences. Only when mention was made of the Emperor did his voice break with emotion: 'I am terribly ashamed that I was not able to serve His Majesty satisfactorily,' he said, wiping away tears. He was shocked, too, that the Emperor should be treated in the media like an ordinary person. By the standards of his pre-war youth, these were 'sacrilegious things'.

The whole affair had touched nerves in Japanese society, recalling the ancient code of service, the shame of surrender and the law of unquestioning obedience to a semi-divine emperor. What part had they to play in a Japan whose international standing no longer depended on military might but on commercial and industrial ingenuity?

Yokoi was taken to a Tokyo hospital where he remained for some time after his sensational return. On 5 February 1972, *The Times* reported him to be in good physical condition despite dropsy in the legs. He refused to read newspapers or to watch television which he considered too noisy. Instead, he watched his first fall of snow in more than 30 years.

A Japanese daily noted that Yokoi was the 3,107,404th soldier to return alive from World War Two. And yet, incredibly, he was not the last.

For many years after the war, Philippine police had reported occasional gunbattles involving its forces on the island of Lubang, and a group of renegade Japanese soldiers. One had surrendered in 1950. Another was killed in a shoot-

Inset: Shoichi Yokoi after 28 years in hiding.   Lieutenant Onoda in jungle kit

out with Philippine police in 1954. A third was shot dead in 1972 – the very year of Yokoi's discovery. A fourth, however, was believed to be alive. His name was even known – Lieutenant Hiroo Onoda.

At a cost of $400,000 the Japanese Welfare Ministry tried to persuade him that the war was over and that he should come home. Search parties were sent out, loudspeakers were used and leaflets dropped from the air. Onoda remained in the jungle, a mysterious recluse sighted occasionally in his Japanese uniform. When the search parties came too close, he fired from hidden positions.

Finally, in February 1974, a young Japanese adventurer named Norio Suzuki went to Lubang to hunt down the renegade. His policy was cautious; instead of attempting to track the gunman to his lair, he set up camp in a jungle clearing known to be on Onoda's 'patch', and waited for his quarry to find him. Eventually, Onoda turned up. Suzuki told him of the concern his case was causing in Japan, but Onoda was resolute. He would return, he said, only if his commanding officer withdrew his order to go on fighting.

Suzuki communicated the news to the authorities who managed to get hold of former Major Yoshimi Taniguchi, a Kyushu bookseller, 63 years of age, who had been Onoda's last military superior. The bookseller was flown to Lubang, where an extraordinary meeting took place.

'Lieutenant Onoda reporting for duty, sir!' said the renegade, dressed in a battered cap and a tattered uniform, and still clutching his old regulation infantry rifle. He stood to attention as Taniguchi read out an Imperial Army order dating from September 1945: 'As of this moment, all officers and men under this command shall terminate all hostilities.'

Onoda bowed stiffly, acknowledging at last that his war was over. And then, with remorseless correctitude, he proceeded to brief his former commander about nearly 30 years of intelligence gathered on 'enemy movements'.

Onoda's story was rather different from that of Sergeant Yokoi. Yokoi had been afraid, and uncertain about whether the war was over. Onoda, in contrast, knew what the position was. During his years in hiding, he had listened on a stolen transistor radio to the Japanese language service of the BBC. He had heard the loudspeaker addresses, and read the leaflets addressed to him. But despite all, he had remained faithful to the code of the Imperial field service.

Onoda had been posted to Lubang late in 1944, as a graduate of the army Intelligence School. His orders were very clear: 'To continue carrying out your mission even after the Japanese Army surrenders, no matter what happens.' When the island was liberated by American and Philippine forces, Onoda went into hiding with three compatriots. One after another, they had surrendered or died. Onoda kept on fighting.

He established a series of hideouts across the 74-square-mile island; stealing food and keeping several caches of live ammunition intact. Like Yokoi, he had known the fear of starvation, and like Yokoi he improvised clothing, using bits of old tyres for sandals. He had, however, kept his uniform intact by patching it with plant fibres where necessary. His sense of duty was even more marked than Yokoi's; over the years, he and his men were suspected of having killed at least 30 Philippine islanders and wounding a further 100.

After the meeting with Taniguchi, Onoda was taken to Manila where he formally presented his rusty samurai sword to the Philippine president, Ferdinand Marcos, to acknowledge his surrender. The President pardoned him, even adding: 'You're a great soldier.'

Onoda's return to Japan was even more emotional than Yokoi's. *Time* magazine referred to 'Hiroo worship'. Again, thousands turned up at Tokyo airport, while press helicopters swarmed above.

The shame and distress which Yokoi had exhibited did not appear to afflict Onoda. He greeted the praise of his countrymen with philosophical calm.

At the press conference he was asked what had been his toughest experience during his long years of struggle. 'To have lost my comrades in arms,' he replied. And the most pleasant experience?

'Nothing – nothing pleasant happened to me through all those 29 years.'

The Palace Intruder

The *Daily Express*, which broke the story, called it 'the most gross and scandalous lapse of security in her 30-year reign'. Queen Elizabeth II of England had, in the early morning of 9 July 1982, been abruptly awakened by an intruder at Buckingham Palace. The man was barefooted, wearing jeans and a scruffy T-shirt. He had sat on her bed cradling a broken ashtray in his hands, and dripped blood onto the royal bedclothes.

For an eerie ten minutes, the man had engaged his sovereign in conversation, making no threatening moves but preferring to chat about the coincidence that each of them had four children. The Queen was finally saved when a chambermaid entered the royal bedroom, took one look at the prowler and blurted: 'Bloody hell, Ma'am! What's he doing in here?'

LONERS

What *was* he doing in there? How had he got into the bedroom? Where were the guards? And where, for that matter, was Prince Philip? The full story of the sensational incident emerged only over several weeks, following a police investigation and the intruder's trial on a charge quite separate from the events of 9 July.

The prowler's name was Michael Fagan, aged 33, an unemployed decorator from North London. Fagan was never brought to court for the incident in the royal bedroom. Instead, he was charged for an earlier misdemeanour. Incredibly, Michael Fagan had been into the Palace before, on the night of 7 June. And for that offence, he was charged only with stealing half a bottle of wine.

At a preliminary hearing on 19 July, the court was packed. Fagan entered with his hands behind his back and strutted into the dock. He constantly turned and smiled towards members of his family. Propping stockinged feet on a wrought iron rail at the front of the dock, he laughed and waved to his wife Christine and his mother Ivy. Fagan appeared to be enjoying himself. Only when the name of the Queen was mentioned did he bristle: 'I told you not to fetch her name up,' he glowered at his solicitor. 'I would rather plead guilty than have her name dragged into this.'

Indeed, throughout the whole bizarre affair, one thing emerged very clearly, Fagan practically worshipped his monarch.

Fagan behaved in the same eccentric way when brought for trial proper. He smiled and winked at reporters, waggling his eyebrows and groaning theatrically from time to time. At one point he even took out his upper set of dentures, grinned and picked a piece of prison food from them. When asked to take the oath, he replied: 'I'm not religious, Your Worship' (he called everyone 'Your Worship', even the lady usher). Fagan was allowed to read the oath for atheists, and read it he did, starting right from the top:

'Please read your name clearly', he boomed, reciting the instructions at the top of the card. Even the judge permitted himself a smile.

Fagan told the jury that he broke into the Palace on that first occasion because 'a little voice in my head' told him to do so. His defence was that he did it as a favour to the Queen. 'Her security was no good, and I proved it,' he said. 'I wanted to show the Queen was not too safe . . . I could have been a rapist or something.'

Having climbed over railings he had shinned up a drainpipe and emerged at the window of a housemaid's bedroom. The maid herself had just returned to the Palace from a seance. She almost fainted when she saw the intruder's gaunt features at the window. But when she reported her experience to Palace staff, they refused to believe that anyone could have made the perilous climb to her window. 'You saw a ghost,' they mocked. (Her story was later confirmed, however, when pigeon repellent from window ledges was found on a carpet.)

Fagan, meanwhile, wandered around the palace 'to look at the paintings and take the place in'. He told the court: 'I walked past a couple of rooms – one said "Princess Anne" and the other said "Mark Phillips". I thought they was asleep so I did not disturb them.' He saw another door marked 'Prince Philip', and then entered the room of Prince Charles's private secretary. There he waited for half an hour, expecting to be arrested.

In the room was a pile of presents for the newborn baby of Prince Charles and Lady Diana. And nestling beside a pair of baby bootees, Fagan found a bottle of cheap white wine. (The label read Vache Tomocula California Johannesburg Reisling 1981 – the bottle appeared in court.) Fagan took the bottle, pushed the cork down with a pair of scissors so that it bobbed around inside, and then poured himself two glasses. 'I was thirsty,' he explained. 'I had done a hard day's work for the Queen.' All the time he was waiting for someone to come and arrest him. Finally, however, he thought, 'Sod this, there's no-one here.'

Despite the very full account which Fagan gave of this first visit, the jury found him not guilty. It was an extraordinary decision: 'Bonkers!' the *Sun* called it, in a banner headline splashed across its front page. 'Next time you are walking along The Mall and feel thirsty, why not pop into Buckingham Palace

---

Early Intrusions

The affair of Michael Fagan prompted the press to examine earlier cases of royal intrusion. A Maidenhead man wrote to *The Times* to say that his late mother, when a teenager, had been smuggled into the royal apartments at Windsor by an infatuated footman. She had been concealed behind a curtain for the sole purpose of watching the old Queen Victoria eating a solitary meal. 'Nearly 90 years later,' the man wrote, 'I still grow cold when I think of the dire consequences if my mother had been discovered.'

If intrusions were not new, neither was lax security. A former Grenadier Guards officer, who had done royal service in World War Two, told the *Daily Telegraph* that he had found guardsmen and police playing gin rummy, smoking, chatting and reading comics instead of guarding the royal family at Windsor. Disturbed by what he had seen, the officer took to cycling silently around the grounds at night, wearing plimsolls instead of the regulation hob-nailed boots. His tours of inspection had their effect: 'Soon everyone was absolutely on their toes,' he wrote. 'But what did the police do? They complained to the Governor that under an 1890 regulation bicycles should not be ridden on the terraces. I was pulled up in front of the Governor, made to write an abject apology and promptly sacked.'

for a glass or two?' it suggested. Fagan had clearly not entered the Palace *in order to* steal the wine, but the decision remained astonishing.

It appeared that through a vagary of English law, Fagan could not be charged with trespass for his second visit; when he entered the royal bedroom.

Much, nonetheless, was revealed about the incident. Fagan, the press discovered, had told his sister that he had a girlfriend in the West End called 'Elizabeth Regina'. The sister had not grasped the significance of the name. On the night of 8 July, a friend of Fagan's told reporters: 'He said he was restless and could not sleep so I invited him in for a drink. We had a couple of whiskies and Coke and played some records. We chatted about children and family – nothing very serious that I can recall. He left about 5 a.m. but did not say where he was going. Certainly there was no mention of royalty or Buckingham Palace.'

It was, nevertheless, to Buckingham Palace that Fagan repaired. And a Scotland Yard investigation revealed precisely how somnolent the Queen's supposed protectors had been.

Fagan got inside by climbing a railing near the gates to the Ambassadors' Entrance at 6.45 a.m. He was spotted by a policeman but, in the first of a startling string of gaffes, the police control room let the warning slip.

Through an unlocked ground floor window, Fagan climbed into the Stamp Room, where the extensive royal stamp collection is displayed. An alarm was set off – but it was ignored. Fagan then went back out the same window, shinned up a drainpipe, removed his socks and sandals and climbed in another window which had just been unlocked by a maid. For a quarter of an hour, he prowled around the Palace corridors unchallenged.

One member of the Palace staff remembered seeing him, but did not consider his behaviour sufficiently suspicious to cause alarm. The intruder slipped through various warning devices which had been badly adjusted. Finally, he found the private apartments by 'following the pictures' along the gallery that connects to the Queen's quarters.

Fagan spotted an ashtray, and thoughts of suicide occurred to him. He smashed the article and, at 7.15 a.m., entered the Queen's bedroom carrying a sliver of the broken glass. He intended to slash his wrists with it in front of the Queen, and made his way in, already bleeding from a cut right thumb.

The royal chambermaid called during the weird interview, only after the Queen had made several attempts to summon help.

There followed scenes of careful manoeuvring to remove the intruder, which might have come straight from the script of a theatrical farce. The Queen told the chambermaid to take Fagan out of the room and give him a cigarette. The servant accordingly led him into a large pantry opposite the bedroom. By now, the footman had returned (he had been walking the corgis), and the Queen

**Michael Fagan,
intruder**

quickly informed him of the situation. She herself took charge of the dogs, while the footman went into the pantry to help deal with Fagan. He offered the intruder a cigarette, and gave him a whisky. Fagan repeatedly tried to get back into the bedroom, but the footman blocked his path.

The chambermaid, meanwhile, slipped away and dashed along the corridors to the police lodge, and eventually a constable arrived.

In the storm of publicity which ensued, some rather off-beat discoveries were made about the domestic life of the royal family. The *Sun*, for example, regaled its readers with reports from Fagan's wife about the eerie interview in the royal bedroom. The Queen, it appeared, had been wearing a shortie nightgown at the time; she had the figure of a 16-year-old and her wig was allegedly sitting in her room. Many papers dwelt at length on the fact that Elizabeth and Philip obviously had separate bedrooms. 'Separate beds:' mused the *Daily Mirror*. 'How important is it to cuddle up together?'

The inefficiency of the security services were, of course, the subject of much outraged comment. *The Times* observed: 'So much for the guards at Buckingham Palace. The ceremony of Changing the Guard will never be quite the same again . . . All that array of scarlet tunics, burnished brass and polished leather, and still an intruder could stroll into the Queen's bedroom without being detected.'

The Prime Minister, Mrs Thatcher, went in person to Buckingham Palace to apologise to the Queen on the Government's behalf. Home Secretary William Whitelaw, meanwhile, faced an indignant reception in the House of Commons, and was greeted with mocking jeers when he announced: 'In recent years a number of additional security measures have been introduced at Buckingham Palace. But this latest incident shows that the position is still not satisfactory.'

Satisfactory it certainly was not, despite all the guardsmen, police, servants, surveillance cameras and electronic devices maintained at immense cost. It was found that Fagan's expeditions were not unique. During the previous year or so three other incidents had already occurred (though only Fagan managed to penetrate the Palace itself). In June 1981, three young German tourists had climbed the Palace wall and camped for a night in the royal gardens, thinking they were a park. Two months later, a 25-year-old man was found wandering in the palace grounds; he told police he was very fond of Princess Anne and had hoped to see her. In June 1982, another man had burst into the palace courtyard brandishing a commando-style knife.

The newspapers dug up Palace intrusions from the past, and noted that lax security was not a new phenomenon. And yet Fagan's expeditions remained unique in their bizarre quality, and the scandal which ensued.

Following his apprehension on 9 July, Fagan remained in police custody, even after his acquittal on the wine-stealing charge. It was felt that his state of mind was such that his movements and actions were totally unpredictable. Clearly he had both personal problems, and suicidal tendencies. In October 1982, he was brought to trial on a charge unconnected with the Palace – that of taking away and driving a car that did not belong to him. Following the pattern of his previous court appearances, his behaviour was somewhat wayward: 'Burn the bastards to hell!' he bellowed. 'This is a Fascist country!' The judge ordered him to be taken from the dock and removed to the cells. 'Sieg Heil!' the intruder roared as officers grabbed him.

Although Fagan was not present for the duration of the hearing, he did leave a statement drawn up while awaiting trial. Remorseful in tone and clearly authentic in sentiment, it provided a curiously sad epitaph on the whole sensational affair:

'Along with everyone else in the world, I love Her Majesty the Queen. I have the deepest respect, the deepest respect for her. I would do nothing to embarrass her. I know she likes to help people and I thought she would like to help me. And I have admired her for eternity.

'I understand that I should have written to her rather than gone to see her, and that by doing so I have caused her unwelcome and inaccurate publicity which I do not wish her to have. There is nothing I could do now to put the clock back although I wish I could. Anything that I can do to make up for the embarrassment I have caused I would do.

'Your Majesty, please excuse my intrusion into your privacy – I didn't realise it would become a world topic. All I wanted to do was discuss my personal problems, but the way I went about it has embarrassed Your Majesty's family.

'You were wonderfully understanding with me and I know you will accept that this apology is written with all sincerity.

Humbly, Michael

In his absence, Fagan was ordered to be sent to a high security mental hospital for an indefinite period. The intruder's solicitor accused the authorities of being too harsh, and indeed, considering how his most sensational exploits had gone unpunished, there was a curious irony in the court order. As the solicitor pointed out, never before in British history had anyone been sent to a high security mental hospital for taking away a car.

Chapter
Four

Weird Stunts

Showmen and promoters survive on publicity, and some have gone to fantastic lengths to attract attention to themselves. 'Suicide Leap' – 'The Human Cork' – 'Man Plans to eat Bus!' The headlines have catalogued the variety of stunts and displays which ingenious entrepreneurs have organized to catch the public eye. The feats of the Hindu yogis seem to hint at paranormal abilities; those of snakepit endurance competitors suggest only mortal lunacy. It hardly seems to matter, so long as the stunt stimulates the thrill of the bizarre.

Ridiculous Records, Fantastic Feats

The *Guinness Book of Records* provides fertile ground for students of the weird, registering such events as Cucumber Slicing, Hot Water Bottle Bursting, Billiard Table Jumping and the Dropping of Eggs Intact from Great Heights. Specially unpleasant events include the Spittin', Belchin' and Cussin' Triathlon.

The breaking of records in such events is generally worth a snippet in the local or national press. At the time of writing, for example, housewife Dorothy Hall has knitted the world's longest scarf (1,332 feet long and using 1,400 ounces of wool), while more than 15,000 people in Austria have joined hands around the Faaker See to claim the world record for the biggest hum n circle (the previous record was set by 5,818 Japanese).

However, it is often a failure, or an incidental occurrence, which stimulates extended treatment in the press. Such was the case with John Berry, aged 21, a South African whose attempt on the snakepit endurance record provided the newspapers with much hair-raising copy through the summer of 1982. Mr Berry had himself enclosed in a glass tank at a seafront funfair at Rhyl, North Wales. His companions were 22 poisonous snakes; at least, there were 22 at the outset. Mr Berry had ordered a dozen cobras, but was sent ten cobras and two kraits – one third of the way through the attempt, a cobra ate one of the kraits. The bulletins issued throughout the ordeal terminated abruptly when the South African was bitten by a young puff adder; he was rushed to hospital for blood tests. For five weeks miserable Mr Berry had lived in the glass tank – but the existing record stood at 69 days.

'Voice from the Grave Proposes to Barmaid'; so it was that *The Times* headlined a feature concerning an attempt on the world record for live burial, which occurred in November 1981. The story which followed was as bizarre as the macabre event. Beryl Wilson, aged 37, a barmaid from Leeds, was to marry a man she had never met, and who proposed to her from a coffin. Mr William White, her intended husband, was buried alive in a grave at Fort Worth, Texas, trying to set an endurance record for living six feet underground.

Their romance started after a BBC disc jockey interviewed Mr White and gave the telephone number of his coffin to Radio 1 listeners. Beryl Wilson 'phoned him and later received a proposal. 'Mr White, who was buried alive on July 31, will have to stay underground until December 19 to break the record', *The Times* concluded grimly.

John Berry, snakepit endurance hopeful

WEIRD STUNTS

The most distasteful feat of endurance, in which various showmen have specialized over the years, is surely that of undergoing crucifixion. An American music-hall artist, claiming to be pain-proof, staged this as the climax of an act in which 60 pins were stuck into him. 'They pierced his hands with nails,' recalled the *Evening Standard* of 1934, 'but the performance had to be brought to an end because most of the people in the music-hall had collapsed.' More recently, a similarly disgusting display was proposed in Nottingham. An unemployed labourer and former stuntman planned to have himself crucified in front of a crowd of 200 people on Easter Saturday. He intended 'to have 7-inch steel spikes hammered into the palms of both hands and feet. Spectators are asked to pay £3 to see the spikes going in, and 50p to see him hanging on a cross', according to the *Guardian*. The display was banned.

On a lighter note, spitting contests have long been firm favourites around the world. The perils, it might be thought, exist only for spectators. Not so. In September 1977, French taxi-driver Claude Antoine boasted that he could spit anyone 'into the ground'. His method was rather stylish, involving a long run-up from a second storey room, the volley being delivered from the window. The accident occurred when he took a running start to the window of a friend's house, but was unable to stop at the balcony. Mr Antoine fell to the street and was carried away with both legs broken, both wrists broken, and his skull fractured.

A different kind of danger, and a different kind of 'run-up', were illustrated in the first annual Empire State Building running marathon of February 1978. This event involved running up the 1,575 steps of the celebrated New York skyscraper, and was won by a former New York fireman, August Gary Muhrcke. He beat 14 other runners in an impressive 12 minutes and 32 seconds. Unfortunately, Mr Muhrcke was faced with the loss of £6,000 a year as a result of his achievement. Aged 37, he had retired from the Fire Department only two years earlier – on a disability pension stemming from an alleged back injury.

Those who have overcome true disability to compete with the able-bodied, present rather more heroic examples of human achievement.

Around the turn of the century a certain Mr Gifford, an American, thrilled audiences around the world with a dare-devil stunt. An unjustly neglected

---

One-Leg Swim Fails
A one-legged French restaurant owner, Marcel Chaletot, yesterday failed in his attempt to swim the Channel. Near gale-force winds forced him to end the journey by boat. Chaletot, aged 50, said he might try again.
Sunday Times

Mr Gifford, the one-legged bicycle diver

figure in the history of entertainment, Mr Gifford specialized in one-legged bicycle diving.

His story is told in the *Pictorial Magazine* on 5 April 1902, which announced: 'Many daring feats have been performed on the bicycle, but nothing so sensational as the performance here illustrated has hitherto been seen. To fall 95 inches on a bicycle would be enough for most cyclists, and they would regard it as a great come-down in the world; but Mr Gifford falls 95 feet and comes up smiling; albeit, somewhat wet because he drops into water.'

The article goes on to describe how Gifford had made his first bicycle dive three years beforehand, wheeling himself along a narrow platform 59 ft above ground, then pedalling over the ledge. People held their breath as he plummeted: 'They fully expected to see him turn turtle and drop into the water below with the bicycle on top of him, but he did not.'

Why was it that in falling, he did not turn head over heels? Others had attempted to emulate his feat with sad results to themselves: 'A German tried it when Mr Gifford was performing in Berlin. He came down three feet beautifully, and Mr Gifford saw his fame and salary swiftly disappearing. But then the man turned, and in the two seconds ere he struck the water made five somersaults. He went into the water with the machine on top and the handlebar went through his cheek. Three months in hospital was the result.'

Gifford himself claimed that he managed to come down straight precisely because he had only one leg. 'When he leaves the platform the right pedal of the bicycle is depressed, and having no foot to press on the other pedal as an ordinary individual has, there is nothing to destroy the equilibrium.'

The circumstances in which Gifford lost his leg were scarcely less curious than his stunt. According to the magazine, his left limb became stiff as a result of an accident on the racing track. After the accident, 'he had the limb cut off, because a man who stumbled over it one day turned and insulted him. Hampered with his useless limb, and being accompanied by a lady, he could not retaliate as he would have liked, so to prevent a recurrence of such a thing he had his leg cut off. He did not mind losing the limb, but he could not stand being insulted.' The article concludes with the announcement that 'Mr Gifford is 23 years of age, and gives his thrilling performance twice daily at the London Hippodrome, diving from a platform under the roof into the flooded arena.'

Nasty Noshers

In April, 1906, the *Daily Mirror* recorded the death of Robert Naysmith, a stuntman whose speciality was swallowing nails, hatpins, stones, glass and other heterodox items. Known as the Human Ostrich, Naysmith came to a predictable end. He became ill and had to give up his profession, afterwards earning a few pence per day selling bootlaces. As his condition worsened, he sought admission to the parish infirmary, and when he told doctors that he had been swallowing nails and hatpins for a living, understandably, they did not believe him at first.

He asked for a knife to relieve himself of one item. The doctors considered him mad, and placed him under close observation. Then an abscess formed on his body – when it was opened, a brass-headed nail was found inside.

Hermit Loses Bet
A hermit who claimed he could hypnotize and tame a marauding jaguar has lost his wager with villagers near Caracas, Venezuela. The jaguar savaged him to death. – Reuter.
Sunday Times

Too weak to stand an operation, Naysmith sank and died. At the post mortem, more than 30 nails and hatpins were found in the body – some in the liver, some in the kidneys, and most in the intestines.

The case of the Human Ostrich ought to have provided a salutary warning to all aspiring successors in his line of business. But it hasn't.

In December 1969, for example, the *Sunday Express* carried the story of 'The Man who is Eating a Bus'. Milovije Ristic, a 26-year-old Serb from Bor, near the Yugoslav-Bulgarian frontier, had bought an old bus and planned to eat it all over two years. Ristic had already swallowed 22,500 razor blades, a ton of glass, hundreds of knives and forkes, chains, nuts, bolts and other items of ironware. Asked about indigestion he replied: 'Nothing a handful of ball-bearings wouldn't cure.'

In September 1982, the *Sun* told how one Alan Newbold's appetite for 'ghastly grub' had led to divorce after 25 years of happy marriage. Newbold was described as the World Nasty Nosh champion. The years of serving up such delicacies as sheep's eyes and pigs' brains had taken their toll on his wife, Mary. But Newbold was undeterred. 'In November,' the *Sun* announced, 'he flies to American to eat a crushed-up bicycle on a TV show.'

In October 1963, the *British Medical Journal* contained an interesting note of Nasty Noshing in its correspondence columns:
'The biggest collection of foreign material that I have ever heard of was published in the *Sunday Pictorial* of September 21, 1958, when it was said that a surgeon in Sweden (Dr Rossman) had at one operation removed: 1,500 pins and needles, 100 nails, 330 buttons, 167 coins, 12 curtain rings, 11 keys, and 176 other things including fishooks, badges, stones, a buckle, and a bicycle tyre valve!'

Was this a record? Apparently not. The *Guinness Book of Records* cites the case of a Mrs H, who in 1927 had 2,533 objects removed from her stomach at an Ontario hospital. A final note on the subject was reported in the *Daily Mirror* of September 1982. It speaks for itself:
Silly Bitch!
'A boxer bitch called Billo had nearly 100 pebbles removed from her stomach after a walk on the beach at Brighton, Sussex.'

Loony Leapers

On 20 July 1981, Mr Mel Harvey, a professional stuntman, jumped 125 ft from the top of a block of flats in Hatfield, Hertfordshire, landing in a 10 ft high pile of cardboard boxes.

The feat was over in a few seconds; his speed on impact was estimated at 60 mph. Was it a record? Nobody knew. Mr Harvey had performed the jump for charity, to raise money for a new treatment hospital at Welwyn Garden City. He landed quite safely, and did not require hospital treatment himself.

Compared with the feats of freefall parachutists, of course, Mr Harvey's jump was a very modest affair. The youngest contender in this perilous field is surely little Devorie Beck from Florida. Devorie was just 23 months old when she made her first parachute jump. It was over 12,000 ft and, amazingly, the first 7,500 ft were freefall.

'Skybaby' Devorie jumped attached by a special harness to her father Jim, a Florida miner. Of her first plunge through space she declared, 'We had fun. We had fun.' At the time of writing, Devorie has made two more leaps, and is quite an old hand at the game, having reached the venerable age of $2\frac{1}{2}$. Indeed, she is so relaxed that she even clutches a lollipop as she falls.

By her father's account, Devorie started asking to be taken on a jump as soon as she could talk. 'It's my turn,' she would tell him every time she saw him land. Jim Beck, an experienced skydiver with over 1,000 jumps to his credit, eventually got an extra large parachute to satisfy her demands: 'If for one moment she had changed her mind or hesitated, I wouldn't have jumped with her,' he said. But wasn't it risky? 'I would never take her if I was not 100 per cent sure there was no risk,' he said.

But parachutes don't always open, as Mr Beck must be fully aware. Take the case of Jonathan Vowles, a schoolboy from Ludlow, who at 16 was a positive antique by Skybaby standards. Jonathan was one of six pupils from his school who were permitted to jump with the Army's Flying Bugles display team, based at Shrewsbury.

Jonathan jumped from an aircraft at 2,800 feet; it was his first attempt. Having left the plane, he pulled the ripcord as advised. One of the lines looped over the main parachute and stopped it opening properly. Then the emergency parachute wrapped itself around him. He was falling through space, with both of his parachutes failed.

Down and down he hurtled, with his tangled 'chutes trailing around. 'Although my main 'chute was only partly opened, it was just enough to slow my fall and when I was 200 ft up from the ground I could hear vaguely near

Skybaby Devorie Beck, $2\frac{1}{2}$, with her father

someone on the airfield shouting close to me to close my legs,' he said afterwards.

'The next think I knew I had crashed through a plastic skylight in the hangar roof and was hanging from my 'chute about four feet from the ground.'

Miraculously, Jonathan's only injury was to a knee ligament.

Although in no sense a stunt, the fall of Elvita Adams in December 1977 was scarcely less remarkable. Elvita Adams, aged 29, attempted to commit suicide by jumping from the observation platform on the 86th floor of the Empire State Building in New York. Having flung herself off the platform, however, Ms Adams was caught by a strong gust of wind and blown on to a ledge on the storey below. A security officer opened a window and pulled the moaning woman to safety. She was taken to a New York hospital suffering only a broken leg.

Arguably, all people who jump from great heights have suicidal tendencies. But some are unquestionably more suicidal than others. Mr Paul Goldin, a psychic entertainer who held Britain breathless for two days in 1979, came into the category of Very Suicidal Indeed.

On 2 August 1979, an unsuspecting public read its morning papers that Paul Goldin was planning a 'Levitation Leap' from 2,000 ft. He intended to bale out of an aeroplane at that height above Ipswich and use levitation to 'float' safely to the ground: 'I believe that the mind can control the body, and I intend to use thought projection techniques to slow down my descent so I will land safely,' he told reporters.

Although he would be wearing a parachute, he said he would not pull the cord. The Civil Aviation Authority declared that his plane would not be allowed to take off unless he wore one, but Mr Goldin retorted: 'There's nothing to say I have to pull the cord once I jump out of the aircraft.'

A 30 mph wind was blowing at Ipswich on the afternoon in question, hardly ideal for the proposed flight and jump. The stunt was put off until the following day. 'I'm really choked,' he told reporters. 'I wasn't windy but the weather was.'

Came the fateful day . . .

'Mr Paul Goldin's attempt to "float" 2,500 ft from a plane, using levitation to brake his fall, was called off after he was ordered to leave Ipswich Airport yesterday,' declared the *Daily Telegraph*.

'Mr Robert Pascoe, airport manager, called police to remove the 49-year-old psychic entertainer. Mr Goldin agreed to leave after he was approached by two police officers.

'Mr Pascoe said: "This is a respectable flying club. We don't need cheap publicity."'

The airport manager had not been amused by the ghoulish public interest which Goldin's proposed stunt had provoked: 'I told him he could levitate himself right off my airport.' The chief instructor was no keener than Mr Pascoe: 'I was quite prepared to take Mr Goldin up for a practice jump with a static line. But I am not going to risk my licence to help someone kill himself.'

Goldin himself was full of angry protestations: 'These people have no spirit of adventure. It's my life and they have no right to stop me jumping. I have tried to use my psychic powers on them but their minds were closed.

'Now I will have to find another airfield where I can make my jump. But I will do it. It's only a matter of time. I want people to know this wasn't just a publicity stunt. I will make the jump if it kills me – and I am not joking.'

No comment.

Fascinating Freaks

Throughout the history of entertainment, physical freaks and prodigies have been exhibited by enterprising showmen. At Bartholomew Fair in 1814, for example, a Fireproof Lady was put on display. Her stunts included putting melted lead into her mouth and spitting it out marked with her teeth. She passed a red-hot iron over her body and limbs, her tongue and her hair, thrust her arm into fire, and washed her hands, not only in boiling lead but also in boiling oil and water – all apparently without ill effect.

Angelo Faticoni was a total enigma to medical authorities. Known as the Human Cork, he performed extraordinary feats of buoyancy in front of students and professors at Harvard University in the United States. The experts believed that his internal organs were not as those of other men – but they found no special evidence to confirm their theory. An obituary of The Man They Could Not Drown was published in the *New York Herald Times* in 1931, recalling that Faticoni could stay afloat in the water for 15 hours with 20 pounds of lead tied to his ankles. Moreover:

'Faticoni could sleep in water, roll up in a ball, lie on his side or assume any position asked of him. Once he was sewn into a bag and then thrown headforemost into the water, with a twenty-pound cannonball lashed to his legs. His head reappeared on the surface soon afterward, and he remained motionless in that position for eight hours. Another time he swam across the Hudson tied to a chair weighted with lead.'

WEIRD STUNTS

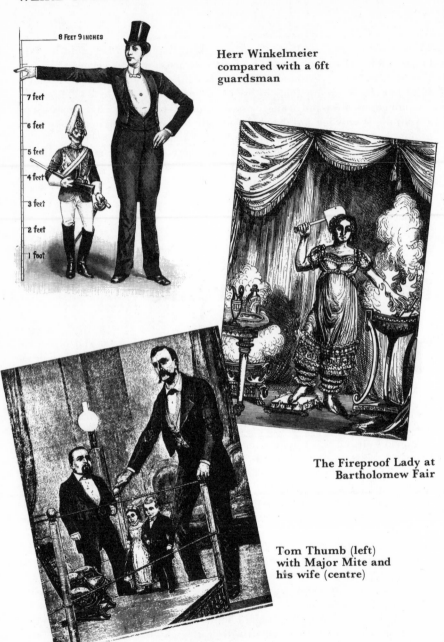

Herr Winkelmeier
compared with a 6ft
guardsman

8 Feet 9 inches

7 feet
6 feet
5 feet
4 feet
3 feet
2 feet
1 foot

The Fireproof Lady at
Bartholomew Fair

Tom Thumb (left)
with Major Mite and
his wife (centre)

Faticoni died aged 72, taking his secret with him to the grave; an enigma to medics and laymen alike.

Dwarves and giants have always fascinated the public. The most celebrated dwarf was Charles Sherwood Stratton, born in 1838. Billed as 'General Tom Thumb', he was exhibited in Barnum's famous circus, measuring 3 ft 4 in (102 cm). His fame rested more on his flair for the theatre than on a truly exceptional shortness: he played Napoleon I and Frederick the Great and went about London in a blue and white carriage drawn by Shetland ponies. Even in his own lifetime, however, he was undercut by William E. Jackson, known as Major Mite who measured 21 inches (53 cm) at the age of 16, in 1880. Major Mite was exhibited in England at this time in the company of Lucia Zarate, 17 years old and an inch shorter (both grew to exceed the generally accepted world record).

At the other end of the scale stood record-breaking giant Robert Pershing Wadlow, 8ft 11 inches tall at the time of his death in 1940. He has had his competitors, however; among them, the 8 ft Captain Martin Van Buren Bates, the 'Kentucky Giant' who fought for the Confederates during the American Civil War and was promoted to captain at the age of 16. Bates's exploits were luridly illustrated in popular pamphlets where the giant was shown with an enormous sword hacking arms, legs, heads and other miscellaneous items off the bodies of enemies.

In fact, Captain Bates did distinguish himself in the fighting, though he was not quite the monstrous whirlwind of violence depicted in the press. He married Miss Anna H. Swan, the Nova Scotia Giantess, who was barely a couple of inches shorter than he. Miss Swan once played Lady Macbeth in an unusual New York production.

Taller than both was a certain Herr Winkelmeier, an Austrian, who visited London in 1886. Herr Winkelmeier measured 8 ft 7 inches. He was asked by a startled old lady he encountered in the streets of New York: 'Mister, were you as large as this when you were little?'

'Yes, ma'am,' the giant replied. 'I was considerable big when I was small.'

No Sex Please We're Crackers
The word 'sex' is shallowly implanted in the moulds that are used to make Ritz crackers, according to American consumer watchdog, Bryan Key. The three letters are supposed to be visible on the salted side, stimulating hungry consumers to buy and eat more Ritz. Ritz manufacturers, however, deny that there is any sex in the biscuits at all.
Sunday Times

A Yogi Poised in Mid-Air

C an the laws of gravity be overcome? From the dawn of written history, reports have been made of people – be they saints, witches or magicians – who have commanded the ability to float in the air. Today's practitioners of Transcendental Meditation claim the feat to be little more than an acquired skill. Enthusiasts for ESP will be familiar with such celebrated figures as D.D. Home, a Victorian medium, once alleged to have floated bodily out of an upstairs window and in at the next. More recently, Colin Evans, another famous medium, appeared to float in the air five metres above the ground in the middle of London's Conway Hall; witnesses reported that he remained in the air for one minute – the event is commemorated in a marvellously weird photograph.

Strange these incidents certainly are; but whether they were truly performed or achieved by trickery must remain open to debate.

Among the most plausible accounts of levitation is one concerning a Hindu yogi, which was reported in the *Illustrated London News* of 6 June 1936. Even to the sceptical mind, the feat remains impressive as a fantastic balancing exercise.

The account was supplied, with a host of corroborating photographs, by a Mr P.T. Plunkett, a tea planter in southern India. 'I should like to impress on you that, as I have witnessed this performance with several of my fellow planters on several occasions, I am quite convinced of the total absence of any tricking,' he wrote.

The report went on to describe how a fellow planter called Pat Dove summoned Plunkett for the levitation performance on his plantation, and advised him to bring a camera. As they waited on Dove's verandah they could hear 'the monotonous roll of the tom-tom' which invariably heralded such exhibitions. The yogi's troupe arrived, and the planters took their loaded cameras into the compound where the performance was to be staged.

'The time was about 12.30 p.m., and the sun directly above us, so that shadows played no part in the performance,' Plunkett observed. 'The compound was about 80 ft by 80 ft each way. In the middle of the square four jungle poles had been stuck into the ground to support a skeleton roof of branches, and standing quietly by was Subbayah Pullavar, the performer, with long hair hanging down over his shoulders, a drooping moustache, and a wild look in his eye. He salaamed to us and we stood chattering to him for a while.'

He told the planters that he came from Tinnivelly and had been practising this particular branch of yoga for nearly 20 years. His family had specialized in it for many generations. He was quite happy for the planters to take

Lift-off – Colin Evans levitates at the Conway Hall

photographs, so dispelling any doubt as to whether the whole thing was merely a hypnotic illusion. 'The camera always shows up that type of performance,' the planter noted. Plunkett also reported that about 150 people had gathered round to watch the performance, further eliminating the risk of deceit.

Subbayah Pullavar marked out a circle in the compound by pouring water on the hot and dusty ground. No-one with leather-soled shoes was to enter it. Within the circle was a tent in which the yogi was prepared by his assistant. When the tent was withdrawn, Subbayah Pullavar was poised in mid air, with only one hand resting lightly on a draped stick.

Plunkett and Dove photographed the performer from every angle. Plunkett, moreover, passed a long stick over and under and around the yogi's body as he remained suspended, practically horizontal, in mid air. Besides the cloth-covered stick, there were absolutely no supports:

'He remained horizontal in the air for about four minutes. The tent was then put back and the sides let down. Pat and I could see, through the thin wall of the tent, Subbayah still suspended in the air.

'After about a minute he appeared to sway and then very slowly began to descend, still in a horizontal position. He took about five minutes to move from the top of the stick to the ground, a distance of about 3 ft. Evidently we were not meant to see this part of the performance, or it would all have been done in the open.

'The performer was in a state of trance, and stiff as in the state of rigor mortis.'

When Subbayah was finally brought to the ground, his assistants carried him over to where the planters were sitting and asked if they would try to bend his limbs. 'Even with the assistance of three coolies we were unable to do so,' wrote Plunkett. 'It was only after Subbayah had been massaged for five minutes and had cold water poured over his head and down his throat that he returned to normal.'

Plunkett stressed throughout that the performance was entirely physical. It had nothing to do with the 'supernatural mysteries of the East'. Even if some kind of aid *were* concealed beneath his robes, the feat remains extraordinary. Quite simply, through years of yogic practice, Subbayah Pullavar had mastered a very weird stunt.

Tickling the ivories
The French Colonel Borderry, an offbeat entertainer of the Edwardian era, specialised in piano-playing by gunshot. He was especially noted for his rippling Intermezzo from *Cavalleria Rusticana* delivered with volleys from a standard Winchester repeating rifle.

Advertising Gimmicks

In 1977, a bizarre legal battle broke out in the United States, between the self-proclaimed president of a non-existent country and the New York Telephone Company. The case revolved around 16 entries in the Manhattan telephone directory under the general heading, 'Montmartre, Government of '.

The entries included the Montmartre International War Crimes Commission, the Montmartre Military Mission to the Kurds, the Commission to Internationalise the Vatican City State and the Montmartre Military Mission to the Royal Scottish Jacobite Government. The entries had been made by Mr Barry Richmond, who claimed to rule 16 million people within a 500-square mile territory in New York State.

The New York Telephone Company was not amused, and planned to cut the entries from the next year's directory. Richmond protested, and warned: 'I told the man from the 'phone company that if I caught any telephone men on my territory out of uniform I would have them hanged as spies.'

In fact, the whole affair was a publicity stunt. Richmond, a theatrical promoter, had plans to revive in the United States the once-celebrated French theatre of the grotesque, the Grand Guignol, which was listed as his republic's National Theatre.

The history of advertising is rich in weird stunts designed to get the product known – at whatever cost. In the early 19th century, for example, a huge, horse-drawn top hat, mounted on springs, plied London streets advertising Perring's Light Hats. With advances in technology, new possibilities opened up. In 1893, a cloud projector was erected at the Chicago Exhibition, beaming into the heavens statistics of how many people had visited the Fair during the day. The idea was also adopted to advertise the *Picture Magazine.*

During the inter-war period, pilots developed the art of sky-writing with trails of smoke. There was even a vogue for sky-shouting. 'Suddenly you will hear a voice from heaven shouting "Smoke Old Gold", and then you will hear a bit of music,' protested one victim, adding: 'It is very discouraging to any mental application.'

The sky was the limit – the ultimate hoarding – and its use for advertising aroused bitter controversy. When asked whether the public could really be expected to enjoy reading such messages as 'Buy Baxter's Pills and Cure Constipation' in the heavens, one irate inventor protested: 'I often wonder why it is that when approaching this question my opponents always think of the most beastly kind of slogan.'

**The horse-drawn hat –
a 19th century gimmick**

Yet the question was not entirely unfair. Newspaper readers had long grown accustomed to the proud boasts of laxative manufacturers in their dailies – why not in the sky? Medical products had been zealously promoted since the earliest days of the press. In the 18th century, worm powders were specially prominent, and manufacturers organized lurid public displays to entice custom. A certain Mr Moore, for example, informed readers of the *British Weekly Mercury* of 29 January 1715 that:

'This day a Young Gentlewoman had a Worm brought away 16 foot and Odd Inches long . . . This, with several others of Prodigious Size are to be seen at the said Mr Moore's, viz. One of thirty Foot long, another 5 and a half, being part of one 16 Yards odd inches; another 6 Yards and a half, another 50 Foot, and another in the form of a Bird, but very small.'

Curious indeed were some of the items advertised in the 19th century press. For ladies, for example, there was a Dimple-Making Machine, consisting of a knife 'with a dainty but very sharp blade, a tiny keen-edged scoop, and a very fine needle'. With these instruments, it was alleged, 'a pretty, life-like dimple can be produced as effective as the genuine print of the "angel's kiss"'.

For gentlemen, the *Penny Magazine* of 1909 advertised the only patent Nose Machines in the world: 'Improve ugly noses of all kinds. Can be worn during sleep'. Ugly ears? 'My patent Rubber Ear Caps remedy ugly outstanding ears.' 'We Buy Old or Disused False Teeth' declared an Ipswich firm in the *Penny Pictorial*.

With such extraordinary claims being made daily in the newspapers, were aerial laxatives such an unthinkable proposition?

Sometimes, an advertising campaign may go disastrously wrong. For several months through the summer of 1982, Lever Brothers of New York distributed free samples of Sunlight, a washing-up liquid, in bright yellow plastic bottles with lemons on the label. The pale liquid oozed out, exuding an extraordinarily authentic scent of freshly-cut lemons.

Unfortunately, people reported nausea, vomiting and diarrhoea shortly after using the product. They had taken it to be concentrated lemon juice, and used it to flavour iced tea, salads and fish. In all, some 2,500 people made the same mistake. Happily nobody died – the director of the National Poison Centre in Pittsburgh commented: 'You'd have to drown in it first.' But the symptoms were not pleasant.

In 1977, an enterprising New York bookstore mounted a much more successful campaign. It placed a large advertisement in the *New York Times*, asking: 'Ever been kissed in a bookstore before?' The ad went on to guarantee that anyone who bought a paperback called *The Art of Kissing* would be rewarded with an expert kiss.

A stand was set up at the shop, and a man and a woman stood ready to

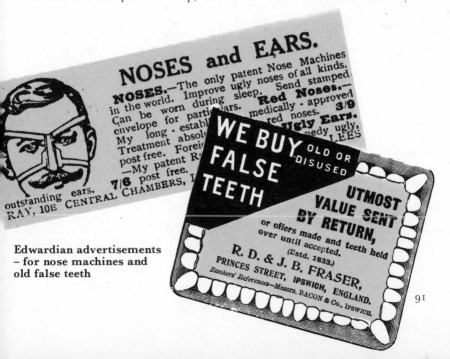

Edwardian advertisements – for nose machines and old false teeth

WEIRD STUNTS

deliver. Customers who bought the book were presented with a paper token, and, armed with it, went to the male or female attendant, according to sex. 'More people came to watch than to take part,' *The Times* noted. 'The shop was crammed with voyeurs, and others were standing two and three deep on the pavement outside, peering through the window. Flashlights were set up, and photographers took photos as the courageous few made their way to the stand.'

Hardly an intimate event, but then it is not the business of the promoter to be discreet. Pan Am staff at London's Heathrow Airport were once faced with a most embarrassing request. In order to 'underscore our commitment to achieve the finest degree possible of personalised service', the president of Pan American World Airways developed a great idea. Huge shiny lapel buttons with musical notes printed on them were issued to hundreds of porters, cashiers and stewardesses. There was no text – just a dozen or so notes.

As puzzled customers asked what the notes meant, beaming employees were supposed to burst forth into song: 'Pan Am makes the going – and makes it great!'

However, when the president of Pan Am flew into the airport, he was disappointed to find that the staff was not complying with the scheme. In fact, only the shame-faced station manager was wearing a badge. 'It's ridiculous,' an airport worker told reporters. 'I wouldn't dream of wearing this huge button. It looks crazy.'

The plan was quietly dropped, along with another of the president's ideas: an all-American college choir singing jingles to greet passengers at the airport.

How are these daft ideas dreamt up? In 1980, Barry Goldwater Junior, a California member of the House of Representatives, put forward a most ingenious plan. Forget the giant neon displays, the skywriting and the multiple hoardings. Goldwater's scheme was in one sense much more grandiose. He proposed legislation permitting companies to have their brand names printed on US postage stamps.

Sportswear and racing cars were already awash with brand names. Why not stamps? The plan was carefully costed out: the fee for advertising would be 20 cents a stamp. In total, the idea would produce $1,200 m. in revenue for the US Post Office.

American philatelists were furious, claiming that their country would become a laughing stock. The nation's 25 million stamp collectors would be up in arms, warned the editor of a leading philatelists' magazine. Again the old objections were raised. What would you get? George Washington's head, and beneath it: 'Buy Baxter's Pills and Cure Constipation'?

The plan was not adopted. Goldwater, however, was very proud of his brainchild. 'The idea just came into my head while I was taking a shower,' he said. 'That's where I do my best thinking.'

The World's Weirdest Geller Report
In 1974, Uri Geller had a paternity suit filed against him by a young blonde mother in Sweden. She did not claim that Geller was the baby's father. But she said that his magical bending powers so altered her contraceptive loop that it became inoperable; she produced the loop in evidence.

Chapter
Five

Religion & The Occult

Is Satan creeping into your kitchen? An American Baptist group fears that he may be. Has the Archangel Gabriel been hitchiking around your area? Bavarians have sighted him in theirs. The quirks and curiosities of religious belief have inspired countless off-beat press stories. Sometimes the tales are merely laughable; on other occasions they have been chilling almost beyond belief.

The Powers of Light and Darkness

In January 1978, doctors in Las Vegas sewed back the hand of a woman, aged 21, who had severed it with a machete after 'sinning against God'. She was admitted to hospital muttering a quotation from the Book of Matthew: 'If thy hand or foot offend thee, cut them off and cast them from thee.'

In May 1977, a prisoner in Wyoming state jail claimed he was being denied his constitutional rights to religious freedom. He stated that he was a Satanist and needed female helpers, flammable materials, record players, stimulating drinks, and bells and gongs. A judge turned down his plea.

Fanaticism, both occult and religious, continues to provide the press with weird tales in an age generally regarded to be faithless. The most sensational case of Satanism in recent years was undoubtedly that of Charles Manson, the hippy 'messiah' who sent his disciples to kill actress Sharon Tate in the summer of 1969. Manson, an ex-convict and failed pop singer, headed a commune known as the 'Family' in the arid California desert. Followers lived an existence of squalid promiscuity; Manson demanded that female disciples copulate with any visitor he chose. The ghastly details of the Hollywood killings sent a shiver through the whole Californian hippy community – in a sense they brought the era of Peace and Love to an end.

More off-beat allegations of Satanic practice were reported in 1982 and directed at the perfectly respectable company of Procter and Gamble, makers of such familiar household items as Ariel and Daz.

Satan is Creeping Into your Kitchen! alleged printed handouts issued by an American Baptist group. 'The rumours are so preposterous as to be laughable, were the implications not so serious,' countered a company spokesman. 'It is very strange the way such a ridiculous tale is taken seriously and then spreads so quickly.'

The allegations revolved around the company's famous trademark, representing the Man in the Moon. Some evangelical Christians claimed that the figure represented the Ram – one of the Devil's supposed incarnations. The symbol was also alleged to contain the infamous number 666, described in the Book of Revelation as a sign of the Great Beast, or anti-Christ. It was found possible to make 666 appear by connecting the stars in the trademark – the curls at the bottom of the sign were also supposed to form a mirror image of the number.

By June of 1982, the company was receiving 15,000 complaints a month

Charles Manson at the time of his arrest

about the supposed Satanic pact, and Procter and Gamble took legal action against four individuals alleged to have spread the story. Ironically, the firm has a reputation of being particularly straight-laced.

Obsession with demons is as old as faith, and has made its appearance in the newspapers throughout the 20th century. In 1925, the *St Louis Star* reported: 'A large man industriously rubbing the head of a smaller man at Broadway and Market Street attracted the attention of Detective Sergeant Behnken.

"Do you feel relief?" asked the large man. The small man announced that he did not, and in addition demanded help, aid and succour.

"What is this?" inquired Behnken.

"Very simple," said the large man. "This poor fellow has demons. I am taking them out of him."

"Have you got demons?" asked Behnken.

"I have not," said the small man. "This bird grabbed me as I was walking down the street and began to rub my head."

Behnken settled the matter by giving the demon hunter a swift kick.'

If demons are prone to make their appearance in unlikely settings, so too are angels. A curious series of reports were filed in Bavaria in 1982. In a typical incident, a 30-year-old woman told police at Rosenheim that a young hitch-hiker she picked up on the road to Salzburg had calmly introduced himself as the Archangel Gabriel. He informed her that the world would end in 1984, and then disappeared.

She insisted that the Archangel had vanished without trace from her speeding car. 'One moment he was there and the next there was just the empty seatbelt,' declared the awestruck woman. Police said: 'The woman was visibly shaken and gave a very credible impression.'

At least six similar reports of the elusive angel had been made in Bavaria during the previous year, and the Catholic Church there was prompted to issue a press statement, reassuring the public that the mystery hitch-hiker could not possibly be the Archangel Gabriel. 'It is inconceivable that an angel would every appear in the form of a hitch-hiker,' said a spokesman. 'And it is not in the interests of God to issue such a message of doom.'

By tradition, it is through the Bible that the Christian faith is normally communicated. Triumphantly undercutting its rivals with a Bible priced 1s. 9d., Nelson's, the publishers, once advertised:

> *Holy Bible – Writ Divine –*
> *Bound in leather – One and nine!*
> *Satan trembles when he sees*
> *Bibles sold as cheap as these.*

The Bible remains the world's best-selling book, and there has always been money to be made out of the Sacred Word. Devout Christians blanched to discover in 1981 that the *Reader's Digest* was planning a condensed version of the Bible, and more than one newspaper speculated waggishly as to which of the Ten Commandments were to be omitted. The potted Bible was published in 1982. In all, some 320,000 words had been cut. Gone were a tenth of the words of Jesus, a quarter of the New Testament, and half of the Old. All Ten Commandments were still there, however, and so was the much-loved 23rd Psalm – only now it was the 13th.

The Rector of Stiffkey

Among all the colourful clerics who have made their fleeting appearances in the pages of the press, none have quite competed for style with the Reverend Harold Davidson, the rector of Stiffkey. Even the name of Stiffkey, the small Norfolk parish he served for 26 years, seemed to hint at the saucy potential of the saga.

The story broke in February 1932, with the news that Davidson was to be brought to trial on charges relating to his moral conduct. The rector had made many trips to Soho, London's vice centre, to help young girls who were in danger of falling into prostitution. This was a worthy enterprise by any standards. What troubled the church establishment was that Davidson had been bringing some of these unfortunates back to Stiffkey – even holding pyjama parties for them in the rectory. Moreover, several girls charged him with attempted rape, or at least 'pestering'.

Davidson firmly proclaimed his innocence, claiming his interest in the girls was entirely fatherly. In the weeks leading up to the trial he continued to deliver sermons from his pulpit implicitly condemning the hypocrisy of the church hierarchs. Had not Christ Himself walked with scarlet women? 'God does not wait to minister to a few saved souls – those icebergs of untempted chastity,' he reminded a packed congregation at one evening service.

'Stiffkey's Rector Cheered by his Flock', headlined the *Daily Express* on the following morning. And indeed, throughout the coming trial both press and public were to remain generally favourable to the embattled rector.

By the time the trial came round, the affair had swept such items as hunger marches and the rise of Hitler from the front pages. 'The Rector of Stiffkey in Amazing Scenes', blared one headline, while another announced 'Rector's

RELIGION & THE OCCULT

The rector of Stiffkey with his daughter

Trips to Paris' – "I Took Many Girls There," Says Mr Davidson'. Across the Atlantic, even, if no other news of Britain were carried in American papers, the rector's protracted trial was fully reported.

A detailed account of the trial is contained in Tom Cullen's *The Prostitutes' Padre* (Bodley Head, 1975), from which much of the following information is drawn. Davidson emerged as an elusive character, part missionary, part eccentric, and part showman (he had been an actor before joining the church). He was entirely lacking in hypocrisy, and made no attempt to redeem the older professional women he met on his jaunts. On the contrary, he respected them. Certainly he was drawn towards the younger women. 'I like to get girls from 14 to 20,' he confessed. His approach was informal: 'He would buy us a meal instead of shoving religion down our throats,' one remarked. Occasionally, on a redeeming mission, he would break off a conversation to perform a tap-dance routine remembered from his earlier days on the stage.

The trial was rich in picturesque vignettes of the rector's activities. But more than once, his seeming innocence was so exaggerated as to strain belief. He was questioned, for example, about an incident in which one of the girls had allegedly been asked to dress a boil on his buttock. Davidson paused for some time. Prompted, he replied: 'I do not know what the buttock is.'

Prosecutor: 'Do you not know?'

Davidson: 'Honestly, I do not.'

Prosecutor: 'Mr Davidson!'

Davidson: 'It is a phrase honestly I have never heard. So far as I remember it is a little below the waist.'

Prosecutor: 'Are you serious?'

Davidson: 'Honestly, I have never heard it. When it was mentioned the other day I had to ask what it was.'

The chief witness against the rector was one Gwendoline Barbara Harris, who claimed that he carried contraceptives in his pocket and had tried several times to rape her. Once, Davidson entered her room while she was sitting in bed with a Hindu boyfriend, the pair wearing pyjamas. When the girl asked Davidson how he liked her pyjamas, the rector was alleged to have replied: 'I prefer you without them.' Did not the couple's clothing suggest that they were living together, asked the prosecutor? 'Not at all,' Davidson replied. 'She might have taken him a cup of tea . . . Pyjamas are perfectly respectable clothing. I know people of the highest character who sit around in pyjamas.'

The rector was a bit of a card.

And yet, to the modern reader, some of the prosecutor's questions were as offensive as any of Davidson's alleged 'pesterings'.

Prosecutor: 'Have you ever had connection with your wife without having prayed first'?

> **The World's First Transexual Exorcism**
> The first case of a transexual being cured by exorcism was
> reported in the United States. A 20-year-old man named John
> began living as Judy and was preparing for sex-change surgery.
> Then his religious-minded doctor persuaded him to allow a
> session of exorcism. The doctor cast out 22 evil spirits, naming
> them one by one as they departed Judy's body. Judy announced he
> was now John again. Two and a half years later, in January 1978,
> John was still John and was contemplating marriage.

Davidson: 'I do not think so.'
Prosecutor: 'Have you ever had it for any other purpose than for the sacred
purpose of procreating children?'
Davidson: 'No.'

Weighing heavily against the rector was what one newspaper called the
'Nude Photo Bombshell'. It showed Davidson apparently disrobing a 15-year-
old girl named Estelle Douglas. The rector claimed that he had been trapped
into appearing in it by two Fleet Street photographers; he had merely been
'posing her for an artistic tableau'.

Eventually, Davidson was found guilty, unfrocked, and disgraced.

So far, the saga had chiefly comprised a 'naughty vicar' frolic of a fairly well-
established type – though with much pleasingly bizarre circumstantial detail.
The true weirdness emerged only afterwards, as the ex-rector used his acting
talents to pay for the cost of his defence.

He began by having himself exhibited on Blackpool beach, fasting, and
encased in a barrel. There was a window in the side which allowed him to
converse with paying customers as they filed past. In one mood he might mutter
sombrely from within: 'I should like it to be known that every fibre of my being
revolts against the indignity of this procedure.' In another his showman's
instincts took over and he might boom: 'Hurry! Hurry! Hurry! See the one and
only ex-rector of Stiffkey – not even the Archbishop of Canterbury can muzzle
him! Hurry! Hurry! Hurry!'

Sometimes he remained entirely silent, poring over his law books and
planning revenge on the church authorities. Outside the barrel, posters
declared: 'The former rector of Stiffkey has been placed in the present position
by the authorities of the Church of England who failed in their Christian duty
towards him . . . The lower he sinks, the greater the crime.'

The act was billed as 'Fast to Death' and the Blackpool police arrested the ex-
rector on a charge of attempting suicide by starvation. Davidson was found not
guilty, and won £382 in damages against Blackpool Corporation. His defence

had been that he had no intention of fasting to death – he could not be blamed for the show owner's advertisements. (Attendance at the barrel dropped dramatically when the ex-rector's defence was reported; customers were particularly disappointed by rumours that Davidson was not even fasting, but kept nourished by furtive supplies of grapes and bananas.)

The Blackpool barrel was comfortably fitted out with a cushioned seat, electric light, and a chimney which permitted him to smoke his favourite sixpenny cigars. He returned to it several times after forays elsewhere to vary his means of exhibition.

At the Bank Holiday fair on Hampstead Heath, for example, he was exhibited in the company of a dead whale. On another occasion he was displayed being frozen in a refrigerated chamber; on yet another he was roasted in a glass oven while a mechanical demon prodded his posterior with a pitchfork. Tireless in his ingenuity, he even appeared clad only in a loin cloth, lying on a bed of nails with a cousin of Mahatma Gandhi.

Compared with such exertions, a stint in the Blackpool barrel was a profoundly relaxing experience – most of the time. Once, his fellow entertainers dropped a mouse into the barrel. Davidson had a neurotic fear of most animals, and became frenzied with terror, hammering on the walls until he was let out of the hell hole.

Considering his phobia, Davidson's final act was one of great courage. At a threepenny sideshow in Skegness, he exhibited himself in a 14 ft by 8 ft cage with Freddie and Toto, two lions.

The act began with the ex-rector standing outside the cage, while the lions lurked behind. Davidson would deliver a 10-minute address to the public on the infamous legal judgment which had brought him so low. He would end with a few quips, to the effect that the lions must be getting pretty tired of his speech by now, and 'I don't know what they will do to me tonight . . .'

Then, armed with a short whip, he would enter the cage for a three-minute stint with the beasts.

On the night of Wednesday 28 July, 1937, the ex-rector's long saga, which had provided sensational newspaper copy for over half a decade, reached its

---

Friday the Thirteenth
On Friday 13 November 1981, Mr Robert Renphrey stayed in bed. He claimed to be the most accident-prone man in Britain. During the previous five years, the 53-year-old bus conductor had been involved in five car crashes and four bus breakdowns, had fallen into a river, been knocked down by a motorcycle and had walked through a plate glass window.

tragic and fittingly bizarre climax. That evening, as he entered the cage, the lions were unusually drowsy. Davidson began to flick his whip at them, encouraging them to 'get a move on'. Toto, the lioness, barely stirred. But Freddie, the maned male, quickened and began to prowl around the cage after his persecutor. Suddenly, the lion leapt and bowled Davidson over. There followed scenes of unimaginable horror.

A female lion tamer, Irene Somner, aged 16, was standing outside the cage, waiting in attendance. 'I got in the cage and tried to drag the lion off,' she said, 'but it dragged him to a corner and we couldn't move him until the lion dropped him.' Norman Wallace, a fairground assistant, described how Davidson fought furiously with the lion but could not shake him off. There was only one pole long enough to go through the bars and it was hidden underneath the cage.

Most of the audience had bolted with panic, but William Bliss, a Watford clerk, watched as the ex-rector was 'carried round the den as a cat does a mouse'.

Inside the cage, the female lion tamer 'grasped a wooden handle, and as the lion came within reach I managed to jam it into its mouth, but it broke. Then I used an iron bar, but could not reach the lion.' The girl, who was holding the beast with one hand, hit it repeatedly on the head with the other and eventually separated them.

Too late, alas. With his neck shattered and a fearsome gash behind one ear, Harold Davidson was rushed to hospital in a critical condition. He died there on 30 July.

And so the saga ended . . . or almost ended. Following the grand traditions of stage, it remained for the show to go on. Even as Davidson lay dying in hospital, a huge poster was set up outside the fateful pavilion, advertising two of the three principal actors in the drama:

See the Lion
that mauled and injured the Rector
and the Plucky Girl
who went to his Rescue

On the day that Davidson breathed his last, the pavilion was closed. However, Mr Fred Rye, the proprietor, told a *Daily Express* reporter: 'We shall be open for business tomorrow. We expect to get a big bank holiday crowd. The rector's name will still be used. We shall have a nice, sympathetic notice outside the booth, and people will be invited to pay to see the lion that mauled the rector and caused his death. The rector was a sportsman. I'm sure he wouldn't mind.'

Crazy Cults

'**A**n Irishman whose followers claim he once restored his pet goldfish to life has set up business as God in a two-storey bungalow in Bognor Regis,' announced the *Daily Telegraph* in March 1980. The article went on to describe how parents and local religious leaders were growing concerned at the support he was attracting from young people. The man claimed to be 'the greatest incarnation of God in the history of man – a true Perfect Master'.

Allegedly besotted followers were required to repeat an incantatory sequence of words over and over again in attempts to summon up a 1,000-petal lotus flower which was said to appear as a burning bush. One parent said: 'It really is a most pernicious organization. It is causing much distress.' It was not clear what part three garden gnomes, squatting at the rear of the Master's garden, played in the rites.

As if to counter the growing encroachments of science, an extraordinary number of weird cults have proliferated in recent years. The sects' practices and

Mass Moonie wedding, New York, 1982

beliefs may appear laughable to outsiders; and yet, to parents and relatives of youthful disciples, their influence is often deeply disturbing.

Among the most famous is the Unification Church of Korean-born Reverend Sun Myung Moon. Amazing scenes were witnessed in July 1982, when more than 2,000 couples were married in New York's Madison Square Garden – all chosen for each other by the cult leader. The mass Moonie wedding took place in front of a football-crowd sized congregation; and following the practices of the sect, none of the individuals who exchanged wedding rings had ever seen each other before. Moon, passing through the ecstatic crowd, merely motioned brides and grooms to come forward together and gently pushed them onto the road to marriage. 'I put my trust in the Reverend Moon to find my ideal partner,' said one bride. 'When he put us together for that first time, I was completely overcome with fear. Suddenly, here was the man I was going to spend the rest of my life with. But I looked at Richard and said simply: "There's nothing to talk about – it's fine with me."'

Of course, unusual cults are not a new phenomenon. In the interwar years, for example, newspaper readers gaped at the exploits of Canadian-born Aimée Semple McPherson. She founded her Four Square Gospel Movement in Los Angeles in the 1920s, and employed all the pazzazz of Hollywood's golden age to spreading her message of enlightenment. At her million-dollar Angelus Temple, services were accompanied by the music of recorded choirs. Aimée would appear robed in white, and parade under spotlights down a circular ramp to denounce the 'Gorilla of Ungodliness'. Once she came roaring down the ramp on a motorcycle and screeched to a halt with the words: 'Stop! You're headed straight for hell!'

Stranger still were the snake-handler sects which flourished in the southern United States during the same period, and which still exist today. Disciples believe that handling poisonous rattlesnakes demonstrates the intensity of their faith in divine protection. Police have not always extended freedom of worship to followers. In 1945, for example, they raided a meeting in Virginia, where 5,000 people had gathered. 'When police charged,' reported the *News Chronicle*, 'the faith-healers swung the rattlesnakes over their heads, shouting: "Come and get me. Praise the Lord."'

'One touched his lips to the snake's fangs as he was being put into a police car. Another screamed and pulled a snake from beneath his shirt. It was clubbed to death.'

Among all the curious cults which have flourished in the 20th century, one has proved especially enduring – the Ku Klux Klan. Developing out of the Southern whites' fear of freed slaves following the American Civil War, the movement consciously sought to create an image of terror through the hoods and robes of its followers, the emblem of the fiery cross, and the title of Grand

Aimée McPherson visits London, 1928

Klansmen in North Carolina, 1957

Wizard conferred on its leader. This book is no place to catalogue the atrocities perpetrated by the Klan in its attempts to secure the supremacy of white Protestantism in the United States. The following deadpan report dispatched from Blackville, South Carolina in 1925, however captures something of the cult's essential weirdness:

'One of the most unique, unusual and important events of the season occurred here Tuesday evening, when Miss Abigail Sanders and Mr Ulysses Sill were united in marriage in the Baptist Church. The symbols and color scheme of the Ku Klux Klan made beautiful decorations. The lights of the church were turned out, and the fiery cross, illuminated by many tiny electric lights, threw a lovely glow over the scene. It is estimated that there were 1,100 people present; 300 could not be seated. Promptly at 8 o'clock the wedding march began. Preceding the bridal party, Klansmen began to march down both aisles, single file, turning near the rostrum and lining themselves against both side walls of the large auditorium, the lines almost filling both walls of the building.

'Next came the bridal party, consisting of eight Klansmen and eight bridesmaids. The bride, who was never more lovely than in the robe of the order, carrying a beautiful bouquet of bride roses, entered with the dame of honor. They were met at the rostrum by the groom and the officiating minister, a Klansman. All who took part in the wedding were robed, and all were masked except the bride and groom and dame of honor.'

Chapter Six

The Wonders Of Science

The miracles of modern science, technology and medicine have inspired awestruck wonder in the general public. It seems that practically anything is possible today. And yet, once in a while, even the greatest inventors have over-reached themselves, producing such anomalies as Edison's voice-driven sewing machine. In our own day, patents have been filed to move icebergs to Arabia. Is human cloning really a possibility? An American science journalist claimed that it was already a reality – and the press had a field day.

Patents and Products

L ate in 1980, Mr Fred O'Brien, a north-country graphic designer, thought up a wonderful spoof. Struck by the silliness of so many modern gadgets, he invented a hoax item of seemingly total absurdity: a sundial for use at night. O'Brien duly sent his plan for the invention to the technology editor of *Design* magazine. The editor was impressed by Mr O'Brien's night-time sundial and decided to run a feature on it.

The article concerning the luminous pocket sundial with auxiliary light-source appeared in *Design's* issue for January 1981, even though O'Brien confessed that it was a practical joke.

Next, the producer of BBC's *Tomorrow's World* programme 'phoned to ask how the device operated. The inventor replied: 'Photo-synthetic sound'. Improvising, he added that plans had been made for its manufacture in Japan. Somewhat later, he wrote a letter to the BBC declaring that the Japanese deal had collapsed because the sun angle in Japan was $3\frac{1}{2}$ minutes out. Nobody at Broadcasting House twigged that the whole thing was a hoax – when O'Brien at last admitted to the spoof the television people were deeply disappointed.

Mr O'Brien's creation had now taken on its own dynamic; try as he might, the inventor could not persuade people to lose interest. A London businessman rang up to enquire whether, perhaps, the luminous sundials might not be produced more cheaply in plastic. The sundials were a hoax, a spoof, a practical joke, O'Brien replied. The businessman considered the matter for a while – and decided to go ahead anyway.

The *Sunday Times*, which reported the story in March, 1981, concluded: 'And so 150,000 luminous pocket sundials are even now in production in Hong Kong.' O'Brien was on 50 per cent of the profits, and remarked incredulously: 'I could make more money from a joke that backfired than from my serious work.'

The *Sunday Times* was so enchanted with the affair that it ran a competition for readers, who were invited to suggest similarly futile gadgets. Readers suggested such items as: a dimmer switch for romantic lighting around the refrigerator freeze-box; humane fish-hooks which would make fishing a more pleasurable experience for the fish (the device involved slow poisoning with barley sugar); an alarm clock which made no noise but raised a flag instead; see-through yashmaks; radio-controlled boomerangs; and a snorkel modification which would ensure certain death in only six inches of water. The winning suggestions were a cat door for the 'fridge; an inflatable darts board for campers; and extra-large bicycle clips (to be worn when cycling in shorts). The

Theatre in a whale, proposed for a Buffalo fair, 1901

A German device to assist dozing in railway carriages

Circular warship built by Russia's Vice Admiral Popoff

latter was suggested by radio and TV personality Mr Frank Muir.

The readers' suggestions were, of course, entirely fanciful; but scarcely more absurd than many real-life patents and products. In Los Angeles, for example, the city fathers once experimented with a device to make road accidents a pleasurable experience for victims. An upholstered plush couch was fixed to the front wheels of a tram, so that careless pedestrians would be scooped up in comfort. During a trial run, the luckless victim fell on the ground, not the couch, and was hurt. Then torrential rain began to fall, soaking the upholstery – the project was abandoned.

Circular warships, theatres in whales, devices for appearing to be three-legged – what has not been invented?

A German inventor, Herr Krenkel, devised an ingenious life-saving suitcase into which victims of shipwreck could climb while others drowned around; he made much money out of it. A Belgian inventor named Vandertas devised a less successful Fresh Air Machine for poorly ventilated rooms. The ventilator consisted of a colossal metal megaphone covering half of the bed. People complained that the great black hole above them gave them nightmares from which they awoke to crack their heads on the rim.

Ingenious flying machines, and passenger services were patented long before powered flight was a reality. The modern reader may smile, forgetting that America's Transworld Airlines applied for a licence to fly passengers and mail to the moon as early as 1969. 'We already have 5,000 bookings for lunar flights. Let's face it, someone is going to fly commercially to the moon at some time,' said a spokesman. Much the same thoughts must have been in the minds of the entrepreneurs who advertised an Aerial Steam Carriage in the *Illustrated London News* of 1842.

Some of the greatest inventors have wandered down the back alleyways of possibility. Thomas Edison, for example, invented a voice-driven sewing machine. The idea was to save the labour of pedalling by converting sound waves into power. Theoretically, there was nothing wrong with the device – and indeed it worked. The trouble was that users had to roar continuously into the mouthpiece – a much more exhausting procedure than merely pedalling.

Guglielmo Marconi, the pioneer of wireless telegraphy, claimed to have found a way of blowing up the most powerful battleships at a distance of some 20 miles without using explosives of any description. All that was needed was that the enemy warship should itself contain high explosives, and be heavily coated with metal. The *Penny Pictorial Magazine* of 20 January 1900 described Mr Marconi's Death Waves as follows:

'His plan is this: He sets two spear-shaped wires on some high elevation, such as a turret or masthead. These are connected with a powerful dynamo fixed on the ground. So soon as the ironclad is sighted the points of the wire are

focused towards it, and the dynamo is set in motion. The electric waves discharged from the wires sweep through the air until attracted by the ironclad, which acts as an electric accumulator. After a few minutes, varying in length with the strength of the dynamo, the charge on the ship is so great that sparks begin to fly from all quarters, and particularly inside the powder magazine, with its iron walls. The result need not be told.'
Devilish cunning – but it didn't work.

No more successful was the cure for fog pollution attempted by the ingenious city fathers of Pittsburgh in 1922. Hundreds of gallons of oil were poured into the river which runs through the city 'to prevent the formation of moisture in the air above it'. The result, again, need not be told.

New hopes for world nutrition were raised in 1977 when a research centre in Copenhagen announced that it had successfully crossed tomato and potato plants. The 'pomato', as the hybrid was termed, existed in the form of four fragile plants, said to be 'doing well' in laboratory conditions.

Unfortunately, the fruit of the resulting plant was a member of the nightshade family, and deadly poisonous.

On the subject of unsaleable products for human consumption, mention should be made of a soft drink manufactured in Japan at the time of writing. Japanese drinks manufacturers are constantly seeking a product to vie with Coca Cola. The latest is called 'Sweat'.

According to the *New Scientist*, delicious refreshing Sweat comes in cans which describe it as 'a health orientated drink which supplies water and electrolytes lost through perspiration'. The thirsty Japanese are assured that Sweat 'is quickly absorbed into the body tissues due to its fine osmolality and . . . is thus highly recommended as a beverage for such activities as sports, physical labour, after a hot bath and even as an eye opener in the morning'.

Some eye opener. And what does it taste like? According to the *New Scientist*: 'In a word, and not to put too fine a point on it, like cold sweat'.

After a can of Sweat, what more natural than to retire to the Smallest Room with a good book to contemplate in peace the infinite variety of human follies. For reading matter, bookbinders have come up with some quite remarkable products including a copy of the *Ancient Mariner* printed on seaweed and an edition of Wordsworth's *White Doe of Rylston* encased in 'a simulated alligator skin and a cover that crumbles to red dust in the hand'. Discriminating readers may prefer an item with perhaps the most unsaleable title of all time: 'The Interpretation of Geological Time from the Evidence of Fossilised Elephant Droppings in Eastern Europe (translated from the Polish)'.

Inside the Smallest Room, readers may be troubled by bright lights and mosquitoes and welcome a handy tip furnished by a correspondent of *Good Shopping*: 'When my husband reads in bed on warm nights he puts a colander

Delicious Sweat on sale in Japan

over his head. He says it keeps off the flies, shades his eyes from the light and lets in air at the same time.'

Clearly there is an opening here for an imaginative entrepreneur to run a line in perforated nocturnal headgear. As for the Smallest Room itself, however, it seems that no further advances can be made. In September 1977, an American bidet company threatened the bathroom breakthrough of all time: a lavatory seat which washes and air-dries the crucial parts of the anatomy, rendering lavatory paper unnecessary. The report, carried in the *Sunday Times*, was a little vague as to how the Super Loo works in practice. Scalding jets of water? Mechanical hands? Suffice to say that it will save an average family of four 50,000 sheets of toilet paper every year.

Paddling Icebergs to Arabia

In October 1977, Prince Mohammed al-Faisal, nephew of King Khalid of Saudi Arabia, flew a two-ton iceberg to the state of Iowa.

The prince's aim was to promote the 'First International Conference on Iceberg Utilization' which was to take place during that month. And the prince also brought something else to Iowa – a vision of what the future might hold. For the prince was sustained above all by a fantastic plan to paddle icebergs from Antarctica to the desert wastes of Arabia, where their waters would be used to irrigate his country's arid and desolate zones.

The concept of iceberg utilization was not entirely new. During World War Two, for example, some of the more wayward scientific advisers to the British government had suggested that man-made icebergs should be used as mid-Atlantic re-fuelling stations. In the summer of 1977, a French company with its own plans for iceberg removal went bankrupt. The prince hit the headlines partly through his own fervent enthusiasm for his project; and partly too, because the new-found wealth of the Middle Eastern oil sheikhs seemed to make practically anything possible.

The Iowa iceberg conference, sponsored by the prince and reported in *The Times*, was attended by some 200 respected scholars, attracted the interest of the American science foundations and the US Coast Guard, as well as of assorted entrepreneurs. The prince was quite aware of the obvious objections to his scheme: notably that the icebergs might melt by the time they reached the equator. But the operation was to be swift and efficient. The icebergs, he suggested, might be equipped 'with their own propulsion system in the form of paddle wheels. Their power supply will originate from power generation units located either on top of the iceberg or provided from ships accompanying the iceberg.'

As for the economics of the enterprise, the prince maintained that it all made sound financial sense. Desalination plants, for extracting fresh water from the sea, were immensely costly. In contrast, it was estimated that the cost of paddling a 100m ton iceberg to Saudi Arabia would be a snip.

However, even supposing that shifting icebergs around the world was possible, there were serious legal and political problems to consider. A State Department legal expert pointed out that several different countries had laid claim to parts of the Antarctic. Governments had not yet considered the legality of simply sailing south, catching an Antarctic iceberg and towing it away. If the scheme really took off, a continent might be partially dismembered. The expert was interested in the prince's idea, but remained sceptical.

As yet, no icebergs have been appropriated from Antarctica, but the prince remains an enthusiast for his scheme. In 1982, he visited the United States on an investment tour. The *Daily Telegraph* commented: 'If Allah is as shrewd as he is merciful he will arrange a meeting between the prince and Mr Anthony Mamo of Arlington Heights, Illinois, holder of Patent No. 4,320,989 covering a new method for iceberg propulsion over long distances.'

Mr Mamo, it transpired, had devised a method for moving icebergs through the oceans by using tiny air bubbles released through perforated tubes placed under one side of the iceberg. The movement of air should then propel the iceberg in the opposite direction. The inventor's patent suggests that the air could be pumped through tubes aboard one or more escort ships. No paddle wheels would be required, indeed no contact with or boarding of the iceberg was necessary. Concluding, the *Telegraph* noted: 'The inventor has successfully moved simulated icebergs in simulated oceans.'

Beware of Robots

At the time of writing there are 10,000 robot workers in Japanese factories, about half that number in the United States, some 3,000 in the Soviet Union, 713 in Britain and about 600 in France. Unquestionably, Japan leads the world in the field of automation, and already its robots are posing problems; one mechanical monster has gone berserk and killed a man in a Japanese car factory.

A robot is an apparently human automaton; the term was coined as early as 1920, in a play called *R.U.R.* (Rossum's Universal Robots) written by the Czech writer Čapek. *Robota* means forced labour in Czech, but since the machines have become a reality, safety advisers have had to draw up guides on how to keep robots subservient. In June 1982, the *Daily Telegraph* outlined some of the problems: 'Unlike other automated machinery, robots move about in unpredictable patterns. Thus in a modern car works they look like malevolent ostriches, with necks and beaks making darting, stabbing actions as they wield welding equipment, spitting sparks.'

Apprehensive, *Guardian* readers were alarmed only two months later by a piece headlined: 'Robot Jailed'. It disclosed that a four-foot robot was hauled

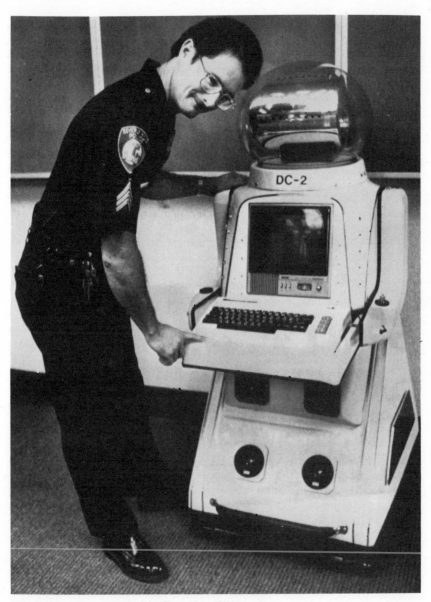

Maverick robot arrested in Beverley Hills, 1982

off to police cells when it was unable to give an account of itself as it strode, lights flashing, along the exclusive Beverley Drive in Los Angeles. A policeman was called to the scene, and when the robot failed to respond to questioning the suspect was taken down to the station in a police van.

A police spokesman said: 'The device was being operated by remote control, but the operator refused to come forward and identify himself – so the robot is spending the night in the station.' He did not say whether the robot was being charged.

Of course, robots are not all bad; many are perfectly law-abiding. Indeed, the latest developments suggest that robot security guards will shortly be employed to protect business premises. Burglars will be relieved to know that one thing the robots will not be programmed to do is clobber. Once an intruder is cornered, the mechanical monsters will simply scream – very, very loudly. And as the terrified malefactor stands riveted to the ground with fright, the robot will summon the police by radio.

The potential of robots appears to be limitless. Already, the Japanese factory of Fanuc, eighty miles west of Tokyo, is staffed by robots which make the parts for other robots. In this, the world's most advanced robot-manufacturing plant, up to a hundred robots are made each month. The factory runs 24 hours a day and has practically dispensed with human intervention. So far, the workforce seems contented – there have been no strikes.

Will the robots eventually dispense with us altogether? The concept appears to belong to the realm of science fiction, and yet it is not as entirely fanciful as might be thought. According to a London conference on computing, held in July 1982, Japan is engaged in an all-out effort to construct machines that will be more intelligent than people. An 'electronic Pearl Harbour' was feared, spearheaded by machines that would be able to see, hear, talk, recognize individual human faces and 'think'.

The robots are being developed by programmers known as 'knowledge engineers'. The ethical question – 'Should it be allowed?' is of no apparent concern. Christian notions about the immortality of the human soul do not coincide entirely with the precepts of the Shinto religion, where inert objects such as rocks and trees are credited with powers of feeling.

But can robots ever truly be made to 'think'? The problem involves much complex discussion. Certainly, as far as measurable intelligence goes, the answer is yes. Computers have, for example, been successfully programmed to play chess at a very high level, even competing against each other in international events.

The First World Computer Chess Championship was held in Stockholm as early as 1974. Thirteen computers from eight countries took part: four from the United States, three from Britain, and one each from Austria, Canada,

Hungary, Norway, Switzerland and the USSR. As in many other international events, the competitors were seeded, with winners playing winners, losers playing losers and so on. The games were played out in four five-hour evening sessions. The top seed was a clever little number called 4.0 from the Northwestern University, Illinois, already the victor in several US computer chess championships.

The organizer of the contest, quoted in the *Sunday Times*, declared: 'Computers are quite good at openings, which depend mainly on memory, and middle games. But they are very bad at end games. They often lose end games from a winning position. Overall, I would say computers are a bit above the level of the weaker club players.'

To encourage computers to develop that killer instinct for the end game, much subsequent research has been devoted. It is estimated that computers will be able to beat grandmasters by the end of the century – about the same time as Japan's incredibly sophisticated talking robots will be at large.

A Cabinet of Medical Curiosities

According to the *Charlotte Observer* of 1926, the Reverend Mr Taylor and the Reverend Mr Dick conducted a learned public debate at Edenton on the question: 'Will the Negro retain his present colour in heaven?' Mr Taylor contended that the Negro's colour will change.

It is not clear what scientific evidence Mr Taylor marshalled to support his argument; the report merely illustrates how weirdly racial prejudice may affect otherwise intelligent people. But cases of individuals' skin changing colour have occurred; and in places where racial laws operate, the results can be disquieting.

In January 1970 Mr Alphons du Toit, for example, a South African White, was stung from head to toe when he walked into a swarm of bees in the middle of Johannesburg. He turned black. A housewife was shopping nearby when the incident occurred, and declared: 'He was unrecognizable.' Another passer-by telephoned for an ambulance. The official at the other end of the line asked: 'European or non-European?' The passer-by replied; 'Non-European – I think.'

Accordingly, Mr du Toit was put into an ambulance for non-Whites and driven to the non-White section of Johannesburg General Hospital for treatment. While the patient was being given emergency treatment, however, the nurses discovered that he was white. Should they carry on regardless, or interrupt treatment to have Mr du Toit moved to the White section? Prejudice won; and in a desperate state, the unfortunate patient was wheeled out of the non-White area and into the White. His condition was critical.

The vagaries of apartheid were further exposed by the case of Mrs Rita Hoefling, a white South African woman who had an operation to remove her adrenal glands in 1969. After the operation her skin turned progressively darker and darker, discoloured by pituitary secretions. A Cape Town hospital worker, Mrs Hoefling found herself being treated as a black maid, ordered off Whites Only buses, subjected to countless slights and humiliations. In January 1978 she wrote a formal letter to protest to the South African Premier, John Vorster, to tell him 'what apartheid is doing to my life and those of others'.

Skin changes may, of course, work in reverse through a pigmentation disorder, Eddie Mae Kearney of New York changed from black to white in 1959. In 1981, she turned black again – spot by spot.

Skin change cases may still provoke strange news stories where racialism persists; sex-change cases, however, have become so routine in recent years that only the most bizarre are likely to feature in the press. The tale of Marion Yerrill in 1977 belonged to the latter category. The lady in question was born and brought up as a girl, and married in 1967. While living with her husband, however, she started posing as a man, wearing men's clothes and using a man's name – usually Paul Jennings. In 1975 she met a 19-year-old girl, through a dating agency. They began to go out together and eventually got married at Hertford Register Office.

Marion Yerrill lived for two and a half months with her 'wife' after their honeymoon. Then Mrs Yerrill suddenly left. She reappeared three days later and explained that she could not live the lie any longer. Mrs Yerrill had been having hormone treatment for some time, and when the case came up for trial she appeared in dock wearing a grey checked suit, collar and tie with short dark hair and a beard.

The workings of the human body are strange indeed. Dora Watkinson trod on a darning needle one day, and part of it broke off and entered her foot. The foot was X-rayed, and a fragment of the needle removed. She appeared to feel no ill effects. About a year later, however, her tongue started to scratch on something in her jaw – and she removed from between two of her lower teeth half an inch of the broken needle trodden on 12 months earlier. It had toured her body through the bloodstream.

Readers of *The Times* in November 1974 blenched at the headline: 'Kilted Soldiers Sought for Virility Tests'. The article described how scientists at the Western General Hospital in Edinburgh were to examine a theory that tight underwear was making man less fertile than animals. The experts had shown that men produce only 60 per cent 'good sperm' whereas animals can produce

Eddie Mae Kearney turns black – spot by spot

98 per cent. 'We think this might be because animals wear no clothes,' a specialist declared. In consequence, soldiers who wore the kilt in the traditional manner, without underclothes, were required for samples.

THE WONDERS OF SCIENCE

Kilted or otherwise clad, people have proved themselves fertile for quite a long time now; and the natural consequence, of course, is childbirth. Babies have been born under every imaginable circumstance: underwater, in helicopters, in lift shafts and motorcycle sidecars. It is not uncommon for a mother, especially one slightly overweight, to be pregnant and not know it until the joyful day. In a recent case, one such unwitting mother-to-be gave birth at her daughter's wedding. A haunting fear common to practically all prospective parents is that something will 'not be quite right' with the baby. It would be distasteful to catalogue the variety of malformations which have attracted the interest of the press. Two cases will suffice, both with happy endings.

In 1977 a four-legged boy was born at a Lincolnshire hospital, and moved to Sheffield Children's Hospital. After six weeks, doctors prepared to carry out the rare and delicate operation of removing the handicap. According to a newspaper report of 22 March, the operation was a success and the child doing well.

In 1982, a child was born in the United States with a bullet in his brain. His 17-year-old mother gave birth to the boy more than two months prematurely after she was shot in a love-triangle quarrel. The bullet passed through her lower back and through her kidney before lodging in the brain of the unborn child. The boy, Daniel, was delivered by Caesarian section several hours later. He was put on a life support system and it was two months before the operating team at Broward General Hospital in Florida felt able to remove the bullet.

Dr Greg Melnick, who supervised the operation, announced: 'He was born in a bad condition and I felt pretty certain he would die. His recovery and survival instinct have been quite remarkable.' The *Daily Mirror*, which carried the story, stated that Daniel was now growing up into a perfectly normal toddler.

A much less chilling case, though distressing no doubt, was that of Tricia Reay, aged 12, appropriately enough from Sutton Coldfield. Tricia could not stop sneezing. On 19 March 1980, the newspapers announced that she had scored a world record for Britain by sneezing non-stop for 156 days; and still she kept on sneezing, on average, once every 20 seconds. Relief was to come eventually when she was taken from her home to a clinic in the Pyrenees where doctors managed to cure the condition. From October 1979, when she caught a cold, to 29 April 1980, Tricia had sneezed for over 200 days.

While various nations around the world sought a cure for the common cold, South Africa devoted its attention to developing a device which would cause people to sneeze. The Sneeze Machine was developed as an aid to riot control, and sprayed crowds with a mixture of talcum powder and tear-gas. It made its first appearance in June 1977. Opponents of South Africa's apartheid regime derived some comfort only two weeks later when newspapers reported that the police officer who operated the device was himself in hospital in Johannesburg suffering from tear-gas poisoning. He had been over exposed to the talc and tears mixture while using the machine on black students in Soweto.

Home cures for commonplace ailments have been colourfully reported over the years. One of the most persistent pieces of advice is to get stung by a bee as a cure for rheumatism; if it really works, it is because the formic acid present in bee venom acts as a counter-irritant. Of less certain efficiency are such remedies as boiled cockroaches stuffed into a bad ear and infusions of mice applied to a bad back. During a whooping cough epidemic of 1982, *The Times* recalled that Charlotte M. Yonge, the Victorian novelist, had the following suggestions for ague: 'to be taken to the top of a steep place, then violently pushed down', and 'to have gunpowder in bags round the wrists set on fire'.

The recent developments in transplants and spare part surgery have created some very weird news stories, particularly those exposing illicit trade in organs. In 1978, three mortuary technicians at North Staffordshire Royal Infirmary were sacked after allegations that they had been holding gland sales. The technicians were paid 20p expenses for removing pituitary glands from post mortem cases, and were alleged to have made handsome profits by retailing them to a Swedish company.

For sheer Gothic horror, however, the following snippet surely surpasses all. It has caused at least one researcher (the author) to shriek aloud in the silence of the Bodleian Library in Oxford. You have been warned:

'Paris – The former director of the French eye bank, has been charged with manslaughter after the death of a man who was given the cornea of a rabies victim during an eye operation. The eye bank was later closed.'
The Times, 10 October 1981

How sick can you get? Very sick indeed, if the *St Petersburg Gazette* of 1914 is to be believed. The newspaper recorded the case of a girl so ill with typhoid that she was practically burning alive. Her temperature reached such abnormal heights that it burst one thermometer capable of registering 113°F – the mercury column simply shot up to the full limit and the glass was shattered. Doctors then took her temperature again and registered 132°F.

The case of the St Petersburg girl is especially interesting in that *The Guinness Book of Records* cites a modest 112°F as the highest body temperature endured. (Readers who find such statistics dull may like to know that the same volume asserts that a 15-year-old girl once yawned non-stop for a period of five weeks, and that human snoring can attain a loudness of 69 decibels, approximating the noise of a pneumatic drill.)

Crash Tests – Macabre Experiments

I t is almost forgotten today that not long ago some curious devices known as air bags were considered possibly more efficient than seat belts in minimizing damage to car crash victims. Some grim and controversial experiments conducted in Germany played their part in deflating the air bag proposal. Fresh corpses were crashed against walls by scientists examining the air bags' effectiveness.

The story hit the headlines in December 1970. At that time, it was widely believed that the inflatable safety bags would become required wearing in the United States within three years. Car manufacturers in North America and Europe opposed the devices on the grounds that they were too expensive, and that their efficiency was suspect.

Experiments had, of course, been performed with dummies – but dummies did not behave exactly like living bodies. You could not crash normal healthy people against walls for obvious reasons, and the next best things were corpses. An American university in fact tried experiments with dead bodies, but they had to use corpses that were up to six months old. The peculiarly macabre aspect of the German experiments was that the bodies were those of people who had just died – they had practically been whisked from the undertakers' slabs, strapped into vehicles and sent careering off to a second death.

The experiments had been conducted in secret by a medical institute working with leading motor safety engineers. A highly respected passenger car development engineer described the air bags' hazards to a *Times* reporter: 'We have theoretically killed people with the air bag. Sometimes it has come up the right way; or knocked against his chin; or knocked his head back and broken his neck. With dummies you would get readings of the Gs exerted but you would not know what happened to his neck. It is not exactly the same. You have to have movable bodies which are no more than three hours dead.'

The corpses, the engineer explained, were unidentified bodies and those given before death for medical research. In Britain, a film of the macabre experiments was to have been shown to a group of engineers in the Midlands, but it was decided that the screening of jolting and lurching corpses would be 'too gruesome'.

A similar controversy raged in the United States early in 1978. In this case, however, the victims of the crash tests were live.

'Save the Baboon Seven!' The car stickers flashed from bumpers and backwindscreens throughout the streets of Detroit in February of that year. The baboons in question were seven innocent African baboons scheduled to be slaughtered in the interests of science. Once again, experiments for passenger safety were at the heart of the furore. The baboons were to be anaesthetized and strapped onto impact sleds that would hurtle them into an object which would inflict severe chest injury. The injured animal would them be examined, and 'terminated' before they regained consciousness.

The tests were to be conducted by the University of Michigan in Ann Arbor. Officials at the Highway Research Institute there explained that the study was aimed at developing life-like dummies that would eliminate the need for using animals or human corpses in future crash tests. The project director was puzzled why the baboons' fate should outrage public opinion. Similar tests had been carried out from 1974 at various universities around the United States. Twenty-three baboons, shipped from Africa, it was learned, had already met their death in the experiments; dummies, computer models and human corpses had also been used. 'This is the first time anything like this has come up,' the director told reporters.

Heading the Save the Baboon Seven Committee was a Unitarian minister, who said: 'It is frightening and appalling to think that people would treat animals in this way, particularly at a time of rising consciousness and concern over conservation; it flies in the face of decency and concern for living things.' And he was not alone in his sense of outrage.

The campaign to save the doomed baboons captured the public imagination as few efforts by anti-vivisectionists had done before. Perhaps it was the surreal quality of the proposed experiments which did the trick – it was not hard for human beings to identify with monkeys strapped powerless into vehicles and propelled towards certain death, while the fates of guinea pigs in obscure laboratories could be conveniently ignored. In all events, the campaign was a partial success.

One of the seven was sacrificed to science, but the six remaining baboons earned a reprieve. Later, scientists at the University of Michigan declared that they had enough data from earlier experiments to complete their study – without further tests on baboons.

Personal Delivery
Toulouse, Feb. 1 – A 77-year-old man entered a hospital here today, told the caretaker that he was donating his body to science and shot himself dead through the head. His body was accepted.
The Times

Cloning and the Carbon Copyman

T he development of cloning techniques received little press attention at the outset. And yet it carried such weird implications that it is surprising that they were not grasped immediately.

Cloning is a method of producing perfect living copies of plants or animals, by transplanting a cell nucleus from an adult into an embryonic environment. Gardeners have, in fact, been practising a form of cloning for centuries by taking cuttings from one plant to establish another – bypassing the natural process of seeding. The cells of adult animals, and humans too, contain the same genetic information as the embryo. So it ought to be possible to 'take cuttings' in the form of a cell nucleus and nurture a duplicate being in the ovum.

This is precisely what happened during the 1970s, when scientists managed on several occasions to produce clone frogs. Cells from living frogs were implanted in frog ova – frogspawn – from which the existing embryo cells had been removed. Frogs identical to the cell 'parent' were created.

Then came the sensation.

In 1978, an American science journalist called David M. Rorvik published a book claiming that he had helped a millionaire to produce clone offspring – a carbon copy of himself. The book *In His Own Image*, became the centrepiece of a public and scientific furore. Briefly told, Rorvik's story was that he had helped the millionaire to find a gynaecologist who was sufficiently skilled – and willing – to carry out the procedure. To carry the scheme through, the gynaecologist had gone to a Third World country with a plentiful supply of women willing to undergo experimental pregnancies. The book asserted that the technique had worked; a child had been born and was now two years old.

Since neither the millionaire nor the gynaecologist were named, the story suggested a hoax. Scientists pointed out that though frogs had certainly been cloned, no authenticated case of a duplicated mammal existed – not even a mouse. A mammal was an immensely more complex creature, and a human being more complex still. The technology simply was not there. Test-tube babies were not yet a reality, and cloning a child was a far more daunting task than test-tube fertilization.

And yet, in a curious way, it did not seem to matter very much whether Rorvik's book was fact or fiction. For the first time it presented before the general public the possibility that human cloning was within the reach of modern science. Might a genius be cloned? Or a Hitler? (Ira Levin made the latter possibility the theme of a best-selling novel, *The Boys from Brazil*.)

In general, scientist agreed that cloning human beings was a theatrical possibility – but that true carbon copies presented insurmountable problems. The human ovum was very different from frogspawn. Cells introduced into it would be affected by 'foreign' proteins, influencing the development of the embryo with their own genetic characteristics. In the American journal *Science*, a contributor pointed out that to stand a chance of creating a true duplicate, an individual would have to transplant a cell nucleus into an ovum taken from his or her own mother.

And quite apart from the biological complexities, the whole issue ignored the influence of the environment on shaping an individual's character and attributes.

Yet for all the scepticism of the scientists, the possibility of human cloning had been established in the public mind; and it left disquieting ethical problems to be faced.

As a footnote to the case of the carbon copyman, it is worth pointing out that a 'cell zoo' already exists in the United States, in a Houston hospital. In this 20th century Noah's Ark, animals from aardvarks to zebras are being preserved at a temperature of minus 190°Centigrade. The animals are represented by cell samples taken from their skin, cultured, grown and frozen. Threatened species such as exotic bats and a white rhinoceros are collected with special care. It is anticipated that the cells will survive for a thousand years – giving ample time for scientists to develop cloning to the point where it is possible to bring extinct species back from their cells alone. And if it's good enough for zebras . . .

The Nobel Sperm Bank

Test-tube babies, artificial insemination – the advances of modern medicine are creating bizarre legal and ethical dilemmas which perplex scientists and lawyers as much as the general public. Consider, for example, those women who have contracted to bear children on behalf of infertile mothers. What happens when one such proxy parent decides to keep the baby she has borne? Whose child is it?

In America, some states rule that artificially inseminated babies are illegitimate. Husbands have sued wives for adultery because they became pregnant by artificial insemination.

THE WONDERS OF SCIENCE

Stranger dilemmas still have been created. Should pop stars be allowed to market their sperm commercially? Or Olympic athletes? Grotesque as the concepts appear, they were raised in a very real fashion in 1980, when the newspapers announced the opening of a repository which became known as the Nobel Sperm Bank.

Like so many of the world's weirdest developments, the idea dawned in California. The *Los Angeles Times* broke the story on 29 February: three exceptionally intelligent women, it alleged, had been fertilized from a sperm bank which accepted only Nobel prizewinners as donors. The babies due that year would be the first to result from a scheme devised by a Californian millionaire named Robert Graham, inventor of plastic spectacle lenses. The aim, said the newspaper, was to produce people of a superior intelligence.

One of the donors was Dr William Shockley, aged 70. Shockley had shared the Nobel prize for physics in 1956, and confirmed his participation in the programme: 'Yes, I'm one of them', he told reporters, and went on to express disappointment that more of his fellow Nobel scientists had not been prepared to contribute to 'this good cause'. Four other prizewinners had, nevertheless, taken part in the experiment. Robert Graham was quoted as saying that of the five donors, three had provided repeated samples. Their sperm was stored in an underground chamber lined with lead to protect it against radiation.

Unlike existing sperm banks, Graham's repository had offered a good deal of information about the donors. Male participants filled out forms giving such details as their height, their weight and many other characteristics. Only their names were withheld. Apart from the three women fertilized, it was claimed, more than a dozen had expressed interest in the idea.

The immediate public reaction was one of profound disquiet. The repository seemed to evoke Hitlerian ambitions of creating a master race, an élite of genius. However, Robert Graham told reporters: 'I don't see any parallel. We are not thinking of a super race, we are thinking in terms of a few more creative intelligent people who otherwise would not be born.' In fact, he went further, cheerfully expressing the hope that sperm banks would be established for 'Olympic gold medallists, artists, or movie stars'.

In general, scientists were deeply sceptical about the whole programme. Leaving ethical issues aside, there was no evidence to suggest in any field – be it science, entertainment or the arts – that genius 'ran in the family' genetically. Obviously, famous families of, for example, violinists, did exist, but the proficiency of members was more likely to stem from enthusiasm, in the home environment than from heredity.

One Nobel prizewinner commented: 'I think it's pretty silly.' Another said, 'What surprises me is that any woman would want this. But I guess people are entitled to do what they want.'

The *Los Angeles Times* contacted 23 Nobel scientists when the story first broke. Eleven said that they had been approached by Graham, and all except Dr Shockley said that they had refused.

In fact, since its initiation, the Nobel Sperm Bank (or Repository for Germinal Choice as it is officially termed), has been forced to lower its sights as far as donors are concerned. Too few Nobel prizewinners have been prepared to contribute samples. Some have objected to the ethics of the project, others to the notions of heredity on which it is based. In a few cases, prizewinners have been too old for their sperm to be fertile.

And yet, at the time of writing, the repository is still functioning. Today, the main criteria for donors are that they should have a high IQ and to have proved themselves by some notable achievement in the sciences.

In addition, donors are expected to be tall, good-looking and physically well built. Obesity is not favoured. Some musical and athletic ability are preferred, with evidence of longevity in the donor's family. Lastly, Graham has named another desirable attribute as 'a sense of humour'.

As for the babies themselves, fathered from the lead-lined concrete bunker, two have been born and a third is expected.

The birth of the first child, Victoria, revived the controversy. The child was born in April 1982 to a housewife, 39, of Phoenix, Arizona. The delivery itself went very well, but some awkward discoveries were made about the mother and her second husband. To begin with, they had both served sentences for mail fraud by using the records of dead children and others to get credit card and bank loans. But more was to come.

It emerged that the couple had lost custody of the mother's two children by her first marriage – after both children were subjected to bizarre abuse in attempts to get them 'to do work and be smart'.

State investigators discovered that their stepfather beat the children with straps, forced them to sleep in the kitchen and on the living room floor and humiliated them publicly. Interviewed by the *Washington Post*, the youngsters confirmed the stories. Both said that the couple gave them considerable amounts of extra homework and punished them if they made mistakes. They said that Eric, the boy, was once forced to go to school in his pyjamas and slippers wearing a sign saying that he was a bedwetter. Donna, the girl, was sometimes made to wear a sign on her forehead reading 'dummy'.

Robert Graham was defensive about the birth and future of his first superbaby. Speaking of the mother, he said: 'She did produce a superb infant, as good as they come. We can't hope to be 100 per cent perfect in our selection.' However, the sperm bank now required potential mothers to fill in a detailed 20-page questionnaire in an attempt to improve the 'screening' of parents.

Chapter
Seven

Phenomena

A Florida housewife's teeth broadcast *Rambling Rose* –
an orb of ball lightning wafts into the Cavendish
laboratories at Cambridge where sceptical scientists
are assembled – frogs bounce off the heads of
astonished city-dwellers – two hideous, shapeless
Blobs are washed ashore from the southern seas. The
world is weirder than we sometimes care to believe.

Strange Nature

Breakfast was a colourful occasion for pensioners Jim and Lillian Barbery. Their hen Goldie laid blue eggs.

'When she laid her first blue egg I didn't really think a great deal about it,' Mrs Barbery told reporters at her home in Cornwall. 'But when she laid six in a row it shook me a bit.'

Stranger still was the case of a hen belonging to Yorkshireman Jack Pelter. His hen laid perfectly normal eggs for two years – and then turned into a cockerel.

From the earliest days of the press, newspapers have delighted in reporting curious natural phenomena, be they sex-change hens or six-legged calves. Among such freaks of nature, the following item is hard to beat for silent menace: 'Salta, Argentina, May 13 – An 18-inch snake, with two heads and two tails, was captured in the town of Saladillo today. One head eats voraciously, but the other does not function at all.' (*The Times*, 14 May 1975)

For sheer weirdness, however, the widely reported Cat with Wings, found in an Oxford garden in 1933, surpasses all. 'I have just seen a cat that has on its back fully-developed fur-covered wings, with which, it is stated, it can fly,' announced an incredulous reporter. The bizarre creature had been found by an Oxford housewife. With black and white markings, the feline freak was prowling around her back garden; later it found its way into her stables. 'I saw it move from the ground to a beam – a considerable distance, which I do not think it could have leaped – using its wings in a manner similar to that of a bird,' she said.

Two officials arrived from the Oxford Zoo and captured the animal, which was placed on display in the zoo. 'I carefully examined the cat tonight,' a reporter declared, 'and there is no doubt about the wings. They grow just in front of its hindquarters.'

Some creatures are born strange; others acquire strangeness through circumstances. 'Mice Grow Fur Wraps in Freezer' announced the *Daily Telegraph* of 15 July 1982, and it had a curious tale to tell. In Norwich, a family of mice had found their way into a refrigerated room stocked with frozen meat carcasses. The conditions were Arctic, with temperatures maintained at between minus 26° and minus 28° centigrade. The mice survived by growing extra thick woolly fur coats. A health official said: 'They were just like little balls of fluff and looked quite different from ordinary mice. It must have taken them several months to adapt to the conditions but it shows how quickly they can change to suit their environment.'

The cat with wings found in Oxford, 1933

The super mice lived on rock-hard frozen meat carcasses in the refrigerated room until they were rounded up by astonished pest control experts. The official continued: 'Half a dozen of these fluffy mice were caught and I was amazed when I saw them. It certainly is the most unusual case of survivors that I have ever come across. They were completely immune to commonly used rat poison. When they were fed with it they thrived.' How they got in remained somewhat mysterious, but it was pointed out that it was almost impossible to make anywhere totally mouseproof: 'They can squeeze through a gap only an eighth of an inch wide by flattening their skulls.'

The flexible cranium of the mouse, however, pales to insignificance beside the discovery made by biologists at Michigan State University in 1977. Their research showed that headless cockroaches learn quicker than their intact counterparts. The *Sunday Times*, reporting this curious phenomenon, announced that 'headless cockroaches can live for seven days after beheadings because of nerve cell clusters elsewhere in their bodies. The Michigan researchers report that the roaches learn to avoid painful electric shocks more quickly than normal ones with heads.'

Freak phenomena in nature are not, of course, confined to the animal world. Giant carrots, monstrous marrows and other vegetable wonders are commonly reported. More discreetly enigmatic, however, is this little snippet from the *Daily Mirror*: 'A tomato grown by miner Ben Croft of Eckington, near Sheffield, had a ripe strawberry inside.'

No less appetizing than Mr Croft's tasty crop were the onions which grew in the allotment of Bradford horticulturalist Stanley Blazevics. His onions grew ready cooked. Mr Blazevics uprooted an onion one Sunday morning, and, when he peeled back the browned skin and cut it in two with his penknife, the layers fell away as if the onion had been cooked in boiling water. Others in the same patch of allotment were also 'done to a turn'. Reporters were invited to come and examine Mr Blazevics's ready-cooked onions. 'I sampled a slice,' commented a *Sunday Express* man. 'It tasted like any other cooked onion.'

Blazevics discovered that a particular patch of earth in the allotment was hot to the touch – a thermometer from his tropical fish tank registered temperatures as high as 100°F. 'I've thought maybe I dug through an electric cable by accident, causing a short circuit through the soil. But that is ruled out because I have dug deep around the hot spot and found nothing,' said the puzzled gardener.

Scientists were fascinated and took soil samples, testing the earth with a geiger counter for signs of radioactivity. The newspapers followed the story with equal interest. Finally, *The Times* announced: 'Ready Cooked Onion Mystery may be Solved'. A lecturer in earth sciences at Bradford University had concluded that the cause of the phenomenon was a layer of compost, about half a spade deep, beneath the surface. The compost, dug in during the autumn, had not broken down because of a severe winter. The reaction of bacteria with fertilizer had caused intense heat; the Victorians, it seemed, had used a similar method to heat greenhouses.

The private life of plants is imbued with mystery. Experiments conducted with polygraphs (lie detectors) suggest that vegetation responds to threat or caress much as plant-lovers have asserted for generations. The case of Norfolk's Weeping Tree, however, took plant sensitivity beyond the bounds of normal expectation. The tree, at Stonehouse Farm, West Harling, began crying in 1939. Tears trickled incessantly down trunk and branches in perfectly dry weather. When puzzled villagers cut away a branch, tears positively gushed from the wound. Examined by experts, the phenomena finally submitted to an orthodox explanation; an underground spring had forced its way up through the trunk.

Much more deeply mysterious is the case of the suicidal trees reported by the University of Sussex in November 1977. Research carried out there suggested that Dutch elms, ravaged throughout Europe by a mystery disease, had not as reported been killed by the fungus *Ceratostomella ulmi*; they had sealed off their own sap-carrying vessels as a pre-emptive suicidal measure.

The Electric Man

The spoonbending feats of Uri Geller are celebrated throughout the world. And yet otherwise ordinary people with weird electric talents have been reported on several occasions, their achievements predating Geller's by many years.

Take the case of Mr Charles Borkett, reported in the *Daily Mirror* of 16 September 1952:

'When Mrs Borkett wakes up in the early morning and sees violet sparks flying in the darkness, she doesn't scream – she knows it is her husband Charles rubbing a 'dud' electric bulb to get sufficient light to see the bedside clock. It's easier than putting on the light.'

Mr Borkett, aged 63, could take a bulb with a broken filament, rub it smartly and then, by stroking it with long, slender fingers, produce a bright violet flash inside the glass. He demonstrated his powers to reporters at his home in Port Talbot. Three bulbs – two with broken filaments and one intact – glowed with the weird violet light as he handled them.

A former railway signalman, Borkett first discovered his talent when his bicycle lamp failed on the way to work. He told reporters: 'I know quite a bit about electricity, but I can't explain this. Glass is an insulator, yet it seems that electricity is being transmitted from my body through the glass to create light inside the bulb.'

An electrical engineer commented: 'This man probably has an exceptionally dry skin, and if he applied a little friction to the glass of the bulbs, it would be sufficient to create light inside the bulb.'

An Aerial Steam Carriage

This is the name which has been given to a new machine, for which a company has taken out a patent and which is to convey passengers, goods, and despatches through the air, performing the journey from London to India in four days! and to travel at the rate of 75 to 100 miles per hour. Absurd and chimerical as this scheme appears, we understand that a company has been really formed to carry it into operation, and that the patent was formally sealed on the 29th of September last. In January the machine will be thoroughly organised, and until then we take leave of the subject, and only trust that this alleged invention is neither exaggerated nor an Utopian project.
Illustrated London News, 12 November 1842

PHENOMENA

The Lady with Broadcaster's Teeth

Among all the bizarre maladies which may afflict a human being, the prize for weird comedy must surely be awarded to the broadcaster's teeth possessed by a housewife of Daytona Beach, Florida.

The lady in question agreed to talk to reporters only if her name was witheld; the phenomenon was an acute embarrassment. For the purposes of this piece we will call her Mrs X – but should incredulous readers doubt the account, they may confirm it by consulting the *Ottawa Journal* of 9 April 1970.

Mrs X began to receive musical radio signals through her teeth on the night of 16 March 1970. Whenever she opened her mouth, her teeth transmitted songs which included *A Long Way to Tipperary* and *Rambling Rose*.

Understandably distressed, Mrs X sought medical advice.

Electronics experts declared that the music was being played by someone using a wireless phonograph to send signals from one part of his house to another. A dentist explained why her teeth were picking up the signals. It appeared that two metals such as gold and amalgam fillings could combine with the acid in human saliva to set up a receiving system – Mrs X's mouth.

The housewife placed an advertisement in a local newspaper urging that whoever had been playing the songs should identify himself. A flood of calls ensued, 'but nothing concrete'.

Dolphins Equipped to seek Loch Ness Monster

In the summer of 1982, the *New Scientist* announced that Duane Marshall of the Academy of Applied Science, Boston, had taken out British patent application No 2 084 335 to further a remarkable project. The inventor planned to use trained dolphins to secure photographs of the Loch Ness Monster.

A camera was to be strapped to the side of the dolphin, which would then be sent off to seek out its target. An ultrasonic transmitter and receiver on the camera mount would be rigged up to trigger a motorized camera and flash unit when it approached something big underwater.

To prevent the camera wasting film as the dolphin passed its control ship, the camera would be equipped with a pressure sensitive switch. This would render the entire photo system inoperable until the dolphin had dived to the target depth.

The exhausted Mrs X then moved out of her neighbourhood and took to sleeping in a motel, out of range of the wireless enthusiast, to get some peace. But this offered no long-term solution. Finally, Mrs X became desperate. One Wednesday in April she had all her fillings but one replaced by plastic. The remaining metal filling was left because it involved a root and might have to be pulled.

The music stopped for three days. 'I thought I was free and was ready to throw a party,' she said.

And then her teeth tuned up again. *Rambling Rose, Rambling Rose . . .*

The music was much weaker than before, but still present, humming away in the last metallic molar.

The newspaper account ends there, with the reporter speculating that so far as the lone tooth was concerned, Mrs X 'might yet be driven to extraction'. I do not know whether the maverick filling was silenced once and for all, or whether the wireless enthusiast was ever located. In fairness, he was clearly an unwitting persecutor. If the couple did meet, we can only hope that Mrs X forgave him – and had no hard fillings.

Mystery File

I t is not the purpose of this book to explore the paranormal at length. Such subjects as ESP, ghosts, the lost city of Atlantis and the Bermuda Triangle have inspired countless newspaper stories, but the elements of fact and fiction are often so closely interwoven that volumes have been written in attempts to disentangle them. It seems appropriate nonetheless to devote a little space to some of the longest-running press mysteries.

The Loch Ness Monster saga really began with a now famous report of 2 May 1933, carried in the *Inverness Courier*. 'Strange Spectacle on Loch Ness' announced the headline, and the article went on to describe how an Inverness businessman and his wife had seen a creature which 'disported itself, rolling and plunging for fully a minute, its body resembling that of a whale, and the water cascading and churning like a simmering cauldron.'

In fact, Nessie had been sighted as early as AD 565, by an Irish monk. *The Times* of 6 March 1856 had reported a 'Sea Serpent in the Highlands'. But it was only after the Inverness couple's sighting that the monster became a popular obsession. Photographs were published, new sightings made – throughout the summer of 1933, the press had a field day. The story has never died since; at the time of writing, a patent has been taken out by Bostonian Duane Marshall, who hopes to photograph Nessie using cameras attached to trained dolphins.

The Abominable Snowman earned his name in 1920. Like Nessie, he was the subject of legends and reports dating to a much earlier period. However, it was after the first British Mount Everest Expedition sighted elusive figures which left huge footprints at about 17,000 feet, that the press really got its teeth into the story. The Sherpa guides identified the creatures under various locally used names – one of which was mistranslated as 'Abominable Snowman'.

Who were the hairy humanoids that trod the Himalayan snows? Footprints were first photographed in 1937; controversy raged in the press. Were they left by Neanderthals? Human outcasts? Brown bears? The most curious piece of evidence produced was a yeti scalp of which a photographed appeared in the *Illustrated London News* on 27 March 1954. It was supplied by a Professor C. von Fürer-Haimendorf, a noted anthropologist. The professor had discovered the scalp among various ritual objects kept in a small Buddhist temple at Pangboche village. Even he doubted that it was a true scalp, however, claiming instead that it was probably 'a piece of hide from another part of the body, moulded into its present shape while still fresh and pliable'. The article was made of tough skin, with sparse, bristly hair of brownish colour. It was later discovered that three such scalps existed.

Sherpas declared yetis to be not uncommon sights, and that they were generally harmless. As late as 1974, however, the *Sunday Times* reported that a 19-year-old yak herder had been assaulted by a four-foot yeti which attacked her herds and killed five by twisting their horns. Nepalese police had 'confirmed' the attack, and a photographer had recorded the footprints.

'I Was Raped By the Abominable Snowman!' declared a headline in the *National Bulletin* of 30 June 1969. The article concerned an attack by the yeti's American cousin, the notorious Bigfoot which is alleged to stalk the remote forests of northern California. A film of the creature was produced by former rodeo cowboy, Roger Patterson, in 1967. Sceptics assumed it to be a hoax – but found the assumption hard to prove.

This problem has proved the most daunting to serious investigators of the UFO phenomenon. It is not hard to set up a plausible hoax, while it is an immensely difficult task to expose it. Strange objects have been reported in the skies since the beginning of written history, and unidentified flying objects were copiously reported in the 19th century newspapers, but it was only when the press found a catchy tag for them that the reports really began to flood in.

It happened in June 1947, when American pilot Kenneth Arnold described sighting a formation of luminous objects 'that flew like a saucer would if you

Alleged yeti footprints photographed in the Himalayas

skipped it across the water'. The press called them Flying Saucers; and a new popular obsession was born.

It would be impossible to catalogue here all the bizarre craft which have been sighted, photographed, and sometimes apparently tracked on radar screens. Occupants have come in all shapes and sizes, from little green men to the 'Silver Giant from Outer Space' reported by a Manchester engineer in March 1978 (it was seven feet tall, with 'two pencil light-beams coming from eye-level'). Wildly improbable as many accounts of alien encounters and kidnappings have been, a few cases remain authentically mysterious.

To take a single example from *The Times* of 24 October 1978 which began:

'A full scale search has resumed today for a single-engined Cessna 182 which disappeared over the Bass Strait seven minutes after the pilot, Mr Frederick Valentich, aged 20, reported sighting an unidentified object on Saturday. Mr Valentich, on his way to King Island from Melbourne, reported seeing a long object with a "green light and sort of metallic light".'

The pilot, the article continued, had been alone in the aircraft, and informed ground control at Melbourne that he was being followed by a large aircraft with four bright lights. It was travelling at high speed.

Just after 7 p.m., the controllers asked the pilot whether he could identify the aircraft. Valentich replied: 'It's not an aircraft, It's . . .'

The transmission ceased. Two minutes later, however, it resumed with the pilot announcing: 'I'm orbiting and the thing is orbiting on top of me also . . . it has a green light and sort of metallic light on the outside.'

Then the pilot reported that his engine was choking and rough-idling, and the object was hovering over him. There was noise in the transmission and contact with the aircraft was lost.

Mr Valentich was never seen again.

Two Horrible Blobs

Conventional monsters such as Nessie and the yeti at least have something to recommend them; even the wildest reports credit them with some recognizable features, be they the attributes of dinosaur or ape.

More nightmarish, more abominable were two hideous, shapeless Blobs cast up on the shore in the early 1960s. In March 1962, the *Daily Telegraph* reported that the body of a giant sea monster had been washed up on the desolate Tasmanian coast. The creature baffled scientists, having no defined head, eyes or other sense organs.

The hulking brute was 20 feet long and 18 feet wide, and its estimated live weight was about eight tons. Though the body was in an advanced state of decomposition, 'the flesh was extremely tough, like glass fibre'. A party of scientists reported that it had a frill and gill-like slits and believed that the creature was 'definitely not a mammal'.

Monster Hailstones
From the *Bombay Telegraph*:- On Sunday last between the hours of 4 and 5 o'clock, a tremendous fall of hail occurred in a village called Condwul, about six miles from Sattara. The hailstones are described as being as large as coconuts. Several houses fell, cattle were slain, and several large fish were killed in the river also.
The Times, 21 May 1850

> **Wormfall**
> A puzzling phenomenon has been noted frequently in some parts
> of Valley Bend District, Randolph County, Va., this winter. The
> crust of snow has been covered two or three times with worms
> resembling the ordinary cut worms. Where they come from,
> unless they fall with the snow, is inexplicable.
> *Scientific American*, 21 February 1891

No less alarming was the 'huge, shapeless mass of flesh and hair' which appeared on the sand at Muriwai Beach near Auckland in New Zealand, in 1965. Australia's *Townsville Bulletin* commented:

'The thing was first sighted a week ago by a Marine Department officer. Then the hairy blob of flesh was 30 feet long and 8 feet high. It is slowly being swallowed by the sand but more than 20 feet of it was still showing yesterday.'

The head of Auckland's university zoology department said: 'You can rule out whales because of the hair, and you can rule out sea elephants and sea cows because of its size.'

How did it live, this creature? How did it breathe? The object was encased in a tough, quarter-inch thick hide. Below was a layer of fat, and beneath it, the scientists determined, was something fleshy.

Invasion of the Blobs? Deep are the mysteries of the ocean. However, readers of delicate temperament will be relieved to know that in both these cases, scientists later revealed the carcasses to be decomposing masses of whale blubber.

The Minnesota Iceman

Dr Bernard Heuvelmans, the eminent Belgian zoologist, had researched and written about many rare creatures during his long and distinguished career. He had studied reports on the Himalayan yeti, publishing his conclusions in *On the Track of Unknown Animals*; he had made it a rule never to reject out-of-hand even the wildest rumours concerning strange animals. For Heuvelmans had found that even the most improbable tales might have some foundation in truth.

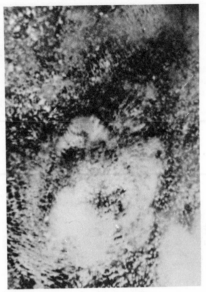
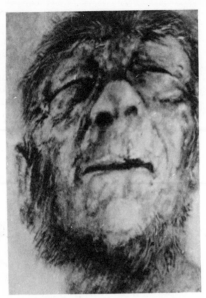

Face of the Iceman   **Artist's reconstruction of the face**

The case of the Minnesota Iceman, however, beat them all.

'Is it a Fake? Is it an Ape? or is it . . . Neanderthal Man?' asked the headline of an extended feature in the *Sunday Times* of 23 March 1969 from which much of the following information is drawn:

'A strange ape-like creature frozen in a block of ice is providing American anthropologists with one of the most intriguing questions they have faced in recent years. Is it a fraud, a freak, or is it a form of human being believed to have been extinct since prehistoric times? One thing is certain; it has two large bullet-holes in it. Just as a precaution, the FBI have been called in.'

Heuvelmans had been invited to view the creature in New Jersey by science writer Ivan Sanderson. Imprisoned in its frozen coffin, the iceman was in the custody of a Minnesotan showman called Frank Hansen. Hansen said that it had been found floating in a block of ice in the Baring Straits, and had been purchased in Hong Kong.

Hansen believed that the creature had existed for centuries in the ice block. This was unlikely. Heuvelmans knew that even if a living creature is frozen in natural ice at death it will start decaying very rapidly: Siberia's frozen mammoths were preserved in bog ice which has antiseptic properties. But as the expert examined the showman's exhibit in an ill-lit trailer, he grew more and more excited. Using a torch to illuminate the creature, he listed its salient features.

The Iceman was six foot tall and covered all over with brown hair. The skin appeared white and wax-like. The neck was short and the torso barrel-shaped. Long arms terminated at huge hands.

One arm was bent at a peculiar angle, apparently broken. There was a gaping hole in the left eye. Examining the creature through the clouded ice, Heuvelmans concluded that it had been shot fairly recently with a high-calibre rifle. One bullet had passed through the arm which it may have raised to protect itself; the other had penetrated the eye. The expert was unable to examine the back of the head, but Hansen stated that it had been shattered.

The feet were not those of ape or man. The big toe was unable to move freely like a thumb and this suggested an ape. But the soles of the feet were too wrinkled. The soles, moreover, were more markedly padded than those of a human being.

Systematically, Heuvelmans drew up a list of possibilities: Was it a manufactured fake? This seemed improbable. A hoaxer would have had to reproduce the hair in incredibly minute detail. The ice, moreover, had been scraped away in parts to give people a closer look. In one place it had been pared off so much that the expert could smell decaying flesh. Heuvelmans dismissed the possibility of the thing being fashioned from plastic or wax.

Was it a composite creature, stitched together out of the limbs of different animals? Certainly there were precedents for such an exhibit. In the 19th century, for example, fake mermaids were commonly created by fitting together the top halves of monkeys and the bottom halves of fish – the objects were known as 'Jenny Hannivers'. But to create the Iceman, the faker would have needed a hairy human head and the body and limbs of a gigantic ape – and where might the extraordinary feet be obtained?

Was it the corpse of some freakish human being? This theory stretched the bounds of credulity. Even the most bizarre fairground curiosities could not compete with the Iceman for deformity.

Hole Swallows House and Car

Winter Park, Florida, May 10. – A giant hole in the ground slowly expanded and filled with water today after a house had fallen into it with six cars and part of several buildings and a swimming pool yesterday. No one was hurt.

Officials estimated the hole, which opened suddenly on Friday night, was more than 1,000 ft across and 170 ft deep.
The Times

A Living Toy
An 18-inch Shetland pony has been bred by Mr Ray Allman, a farmer of Madley Heath, North Staffordshire.
Daily Telegraph

Was it then some unknown species of Homo Sapiens – even a surviving Neanderthaler? Neanderthal Man was a species of early man which existed before Homo Sapiens evolved. The Iceman had the long arms, short neck, barrel chest, and large hands and feet associated with early hominids. The feet, with their long second and third digits, were especially reminiscent of what was known of Neanderthalers.

Incredible as the proposition appeared, Dr Heuvelmans found himself tormented. For many nights after he viewed the exhibit he could not sleep. Since the creature had clearly been shot in recent years, it seemed to reinforce theories that a race of unknown hominids existed in the remoter parts of Asia.

The expert was anxious to buy the Iceman, but Hansen was reluctant to part with it. Heuvelmans turned to the Smithsonian Institute in Washington, who took an immediate interest and an investigating team was set up. Heuvelmans, meanwhile, published his findings in Belgium, provoking intense enthusiasm among his colleagues. Also interested were the FBI – for if something like a human being had been shot and killed, a capital crime might have been committed.

It seemed that the anthropological world was on the verge of one of the most exciting discoveries ever made in the study of man. And then, a veil of mystery descended over the affair.

Frank Hansen claimed that the Iceman was the property of a wealthy, unidentified man. The owner took possession of it, and only allowed a replica to be exhibited in future. The Smithsonian Institute were allowed to see the model – but not the original. They concluded that a hoax was being perpetrated while the FBI declared that there was not enough evidence for them to proceed either.

Hansen, meanwhile, took an exhibit (it was not clear whether it was the original or the replica) to Canada to show at provincial fairs. On the way back to the United States, customs officials seized it. They stated that Hansen did not have the proper documentation to return a 'hominid' to the country. The showman described it as a 'fabricated illusion', the customs officials asked to see core samples.

Hansen refused, on the grounds that removing samples would ruin his exhibit. Eventually, after telephoning his senator and a lawyer, he managed to get the creature back to the United States without an investigation, and continued to show the Iceman at carnivals for some months. But the showman alleged that his contract to display the object ran out in the spring of 1970. Thereafter, the owner took possession, and the exhibit was withdrawn from public view.

The lack of positive evidence has made most zoologists conclude that the Iceman must have been a clever fake. Heuvelmans, however, remains convinced that there was something more to the frozen creature he examined in the torch-lit trailer. An aura of mystery still lingers about the whole affair.

They Came from the Sky!

In July 1982, a Winnipeg man heard an almighty crash at his home. It was as if the roof had exploded. Hurrying into his hallway, he saw a sinister black disc amid the chaos of dust and splintered wood.

It was a wheel from a Canadian DC-4 freighter, which landed safely at Winnipeg Airport a few minutes later. Investigators said the accident was very rare.

All kinds of bizarre objects have been reported to drop from the skies – from monster hailstones to blocks of frozen urine. But the most remarkable falls have concerned living creatures – fish, frogs, and even worms. They have been so commonly reported, in fact, that they have scarcely been deemed worthy of more than a snippet in the newspapers. The *Scientific American* of 12 July 1873,

---

The Finger of Fate
In the summer of 1982, a dream came true for Mr Howard Hewitt of Lyndhurst, Hampshire. A golfer of 12 years standing, Mr Hewitt holed in one on his home course in the New Forest.

On the following day at the nearby Bramshaw Club, Mr Hewitt holed in one again.

As he stood on the green with his colleagues, discussing the extraordinary double phenomenon, a third event occurred. A ball from an adjoining fairway struck him on the back of the head and laid him out cold.

PHENOMENA

for example, noted: 'A shower of frogs which darkened the air and covered the ground for a long distance is the reported result of a recent rainstorm in Kansas City, Mo.' A North African event drew an even terser statement from the *Sunday Times* of 18 December 1977: 'It was raining frogs in the Moroccan Sahara last week. Freak whirlwinds are blamed.'

Those 'freak whirlwinds' have commonly been blamed for fishfalls too. Slithering cascades were reported in Singapore in 1861, following an earthquake: torrents of fish fell in the streets and were collected by the bucketful. Sceptics believed that the fish had in fact issued from the flood waters of swollen rivers, but one reporter found fish in his own walled courtyard which the flood waters could not penetrate. And the incident is not unique. In July 1959, a rain of fish was reported at Townsville airport in Australia.

Wormfalls are scarcely less remarkable. The authoritative journal, *Nature*, recorded on 2 March 1876:

'The *Morgenblad* of Christiania states that a singular phenomenon was observed there after a recent violent storm. A number of worms were found crawling on the snow, and it was impossible to find the places from which they had issued, everything being frozen in the vicinity. Similar circumstances were reported from several places in Norway.'

An almost identical phenomenon was noted in Virginia by the *Scientific American* of 21 February 1891. It is possible, of course, that the worms had not fallen with the snow, but emerged from dormancy in the earth with the sudden change in climate. This theory has often been used by sceptical scientists to explain frogfalls – though it can scarcely satisfy the Birmingham case of June 1954, when witnesses saw hundreds of little frogs bouncing off people's heads.

American journalist Charles Fort rejected both freak whirlwind and dormancy theories. An obsessive collector of newspaper snippets concerning strange events, Fort believed in a multi-dimensional universe and detected the dark laughter of the gods in such occurrences. In *The Book of the Damned*, published in 1919, he attempted a reasoned statement of his beliefs. Falling objects, he suggested, might come from 'a region somewhere above the earth's surface in which gravitation is inoperative'. Into this mysterious zone, objects were sucked from the ground, to be shaken down later by storms.

Certainly, some falls have appeared to deny orthodox analysis. What to make, for example, of the rains of blood occasionally reported in mediaeval Europe? Precisely such an event occurred in Britain on the night of 30 June 1968. The bloody deluge, however, proved capable of scientific explanation. The red rain was found to be composed of fine sand picked up by dust storms in the Sahara and carried northward in the upper air to fall over Britain during a thunderstorm.

Wanted
Extraterrestrials. Researcher wants to meet people from other planets or space-time continuums. Please write with details. Confidentiality guaranteed.
The *Guardian*

Fires from Nowhere

I f there is a growth area in present-day writing about mysterious events, it is surely the field of spontaneous human combustion. Certain human beings are alleged to have burst into flames for no scientifically explicable reason. The case of Dr John Irving Bentley has received much attention. Apparently, on 5 December 1966, the doctor's remains were found in his bathroom at Coudersport, Pennsylvania. The only evidence of a fire was a blackened hole in the floor, a heap of ash, and the charred remains of the doctor's leg. Investigators were perplexed since no faulty heating or electrical equipment was present. It was true that the doctor was a pipe-smoker, but how could a fire capable of consuming a whole man be generated by a fragment of hot ash? The conflagration had extended only around the area where the leg was found. Those who believe in the paranormal regard it as a clear case of spontaneous human combustion.

The phenomenon is not new. Dickens's Bleak House, for example, contains a fictional account of a similar episode, while the *New York Sun* of 2 February 1932 reported:

'Bladenboro, N. Carolina: Fires, which apparently spring from nowhere, consuming the household effects of C.H. Williamson, here, have placed this community in a state of excitement, and continue to burn. Saturday, a window shade and curtain burned in the Williamson home. Since then, fire has burst out in five rooms. Five window shades, bed coverings, tablecloths, and other effects have suddenly burst into flames, under the noses of the watchers. Williamson's daughter stood in the middle of the floor with no fire near her. Suddenly her dress ignited. That was too much, and household goods were removed from the house.'

If a rational explanation for such events does exist, it may revolve around the curious phenomenon known as ball lightning – lightning which appears in the shape of a sphere, and behaves in remarkable ways.

· A dramatic and characteristic ball lightning event is recorded in the authoritative scientific journal *Nature* of 15 April 1976. The episode was reported by a housewife to have occurred during a heavy thunderstorm in the Midlands area of England on 8 August the previous year.

She was in her kitchen at about 7.45 p.m., when a ball of light appeared over her cooker. The sphere was about 10 cm across and surrounded by a flaming bluish halo. The ball moved straight towards her at an estimated height of 95 cm from the ground. She felt burning heat and noticed a singeing smell. There was a sound something like a rattle:

'The ball seemed to hit me below the belt, as it were, and I automatically brushed it away from me and it just disappeared. Where I brushed it away there appeared a redness and swelling on my left hand. It seemed as if my gold wedding ring was burning into my finger.'

Where the ball struck her, the woman's clothing was damaged. There was a hole in her dress and tights. Her legs were not actually burned, but became red and numb.

The doctor who recorded the case noted that the ball exploded with a bang, but the woman was not sure whether it exploded at the exact time at which she touched it. He concluded: 'Before my contact with her, the witness had had no acquaintance with the phenomenon of ball lightning.'

Strangely enough, many scientists still doubt the very existence of ball lightning. In August 1982, it looked as if even the most sceptical might revise their opinion. A ball of lightning struck the Cavendish Laboratories at Cambridge, an establishment internationally renowned for the many Nobel prizewinners it has housed.

Sir Brian Pippard, a distinguished physicist, collected many eye-witness accounts from among the staff and sent them off to *Nature* journal. 'It was most remarkable.' he stated. 'It went through a window as a secretary was closing it and passed by, without singeing her hair.'

A delightful irony – would scientists now recognize the existence of ball lightning? 'Well,' said Pippard, 'none of *us* actually saw it . . .'

Chapter
Eight

Death & Burial

It may come as a bolt of lightning or as a morsel of food. But if one thing is certain in this life it is death. Or is it? Corpses rising from undertakers' slabs – body freezing for suspended animation – sensational reports have sometimes appeared to challenge the finality of demise. Bizarre burials, moreover, have challenged the traditional dignity of death. Can we be blamed for finding the subject fascinating? Death at least is democratic, and comes to all in the end.

In the Midst of Life . . .

At the funeral of a Georgia grandmother, held at Blairsville in July 1982, the preacher concluded a moving address with the words: 'We never know what is going to happen next.'

Seconds later, a bolt of lightning struck the grieving grandson, Donald Metcalf. He was killed instantly.

'I have never witnessed anything like that in 30 years of preaching,' said the astonished Reverend Ray Hewitt.

From the earliest days of newspaper publishing, the press has dwelt with terrible fascination on circumstances of sudden and curious death. Human interest in the subject is timeless.

Readers who consider the modern press sensational in reporting misfortune would do well to consider how our Victorian forbears treated the subject. Not content with the occasional feature, some periodicals specialized in catastrophe. A Sunday newspaper called the *Death Warrant*, launched in January 1840, offered its readers a:

'Reprinted Record of Facts – compiled from authentic sources, of the most dreadful battles by Sea and Land; Horrible and Mysterious Murders and Suicides, Plagues, Pestilences, Famines, Earthquakes, Storms, Shipwrecks, Conflagrations, Death-Beds, and every other appalling Calamity incidental to the Life of Man, exceeding in intensity and agonizing interest any work ever published; showing how Man is dazzled and betrayed by the Vanities of the World, and that the real occurrences of this life far surpass, in an extraordinary degree, any Events which can possibly be depicted in the pages of Fiction and Romance . . .

'The Death Warrant will achieve for the People a Grand Moral Lesson, it will inevitably strike Terror into the Hearts and Minds of Thousands, and bring back to their Memories the too often forgotten but solemn admonition, "In the Midst of Life we are in Death."'

This chapter makes no such bold claims, but presents a modest catalogue of unhappy endings. For example:

A Judicial Error

While demonstrating how a revolver could have been used by the defendant on trial in a shooting case, Judge D.F. Sotomayor of a Tijuana court shot himself behind the left ear. He died an hour later. The judge had been under the impression that court officials had removed the cartridges.

Actress killed by Press Cuttings

A pile of bound press cuttings and other material toppled onto Miss Eleanor

Barry, aged 70, a former actress, in the New York home she shared with her sister. Police said the house was filled with towers of books, newspapers, shopping bags and assorted papers.

Baptism of Death

While celebrating the joyous ritual of rebirth at a river baptism in western Columbia, seven Adventists were swept away by strong currents and drowned.

Goalkeeper Shot Dead during Friendly

South African goalkeeper Mwakhe Sithole met his end during a weekend friendly soccer match. His team, Royal Central, was leading Nongoma Fighters by two nil at the time. Shots rang out behind the goalmouth. Sithole crumpled and fell.

Delayed Reaction

A Lewisham man died in an epileptic fit. The inquest heard how he had suffered from fits ever since an organ-grinder's monkey jumped on him 19 years earlier.

Undertaker Overcome

A 50-year-old Turkish undertaker was killed when a tree branch he was cutting for a coffin fell on his head.

The case of the Turkish undertaker illustrates the improbable occupational hazard to which unsuspecting tradespeople may be prone. Postmen, of course, are very familiar with moments of apprehension as they approach houses known to contain dogs. There cannot be many postmen, however, who have been eaten by a shark. This was the melancholy fate which befell one Tongan islander as he carried out his chore, the circumstances, however, require a little explanation.

Tin Can Island is the most remote of the Tongan group and has for many years operated a unique mail service. Until recently, letters were dropped to the islanders in sealed containers which were collected a mile offshore by swimming postmen. On one occasion, however, a postman was taken by a shark. Since that day, technology has transformed the islands postal service. The postmen now use canoes.

Sometimes the circumstances of a demise are so bizarre that they warrant extended treatment in the press, it almost appears as if the fates had conspired to arrange a fitting end for the victim. Consider, for example, the case of the bad-tempered golfer reported in 1982.

All the Sevens
On the seventh day of the seventh month (July) 1977, a certain Mrs Severn became 77.

DEATH & BURIAL

The man was an unpopular figure at the Sun Creek golf club near New Orleans. So many members had shied away from him that he often had to go round the course by himself. He would hurl his putter into the lake after a bad clip, smash his ball wildly in any direction after slicing or hooking a drive. After the smallest errors, he would curse at the top of his voice.

On one occasion in May 1982, however, the man was invited to join three members who were seeking to make up a foursome. For ten holes, his temper held and his behaviour was beyond reproach. Then, on the 11th tee, he sliced a drive awkwardly, the ball disappearing into a thicket. This was too much – the old rage rose again in his gorge. He ranted. He raved. He hurled his club against a nearby motorized caddy cart.

The club head snapped off on impact and the broken shaft bounced back. The jagged end pierced his jugular vein like a spear, and he died on the way to hospital.

Equally ironic was the very different case of a Polish immigrant to Britain, whose inquest was held on 8 January 1973. This man lived in terror of vampires.

A retired pottery-worker, the Pole had come to Britain some 25 years earlier. At the inquest, his landlady said: 'He thought vampires were everywhere. He used salt, pepper and garlic to keep them away.' A police officer went further, describing the man's lodgings as looking like 'a real Dracula's Castle':

'In the room was a ritual distribution of objects as antidotes against vampires. There was a bag of salt to the left of the dead man's face, one between his legs and other containers scattered around the room. Salt was also sprinkled on his blanket. There was a strong smell of garlic in the room. Outside his window was a washing bowl containing cloves of garlic. From a book, *The Natural History of the Vampire*, I found that these things were some of the methods used as a precaution against vampires. Apparently it was a Bulgarian custom, but there was no evidence that this man had been attacked.'

So terrified was the immigrant of vampires that he had even stuffed garlic into the keyhole of his room. As a last precaution before he retired to bed, he had also placed a clove of garlic in his mouth.

The man choked to death on the garlic.

Kidneys to Buy Home
A 21-year-old Brazilian girl with two extra kidneys is hoping to sell them to buy a house for her five orphaned brothers. The girl, Odete Lopes, hopes to sell them for about £16,000 each.
The *Sunday Times*

Unusual Undertakings

The melancholy responsibilities of the undertaker have conferred a special dignity on his profession, at least as far as outward appearances are concerned. Once in a while, however, even morticians have been known to let the mask slip and reveal their flawed humanity.

In January 1965, a 70-year-old woman was knocked down by a car on a highway in Nashville, Tennessee. A bystander telephoned the police, who sent for an ambulance from the Madison Funeral Home. In Nashville there are several funeral homes which operate ambulance services; every crash victim is, after all, a potential customer.

Before the Madison driver arrived, vehicles from two other funeral homes reached the scene. The rival attendants both claimed the victim. Allegedly, what began as a squabble turned into a fight. Blows were exchanged, and one attendant tried to wrest the unconscious woman from the other. The police turned up and a free-for-all developed.

Eventually, the Madison driver arrived, and at last the unfortunate woman was rushed to Vanderbilt hospital. Her condition was critical.

A slightly more dignified image of the motorized undertaker is provided by this advertisement, placed in the *Waterloo Courier* of 1925. Ed Kistner may not have been much of a poet, but clearly his heart was in the right place:

> *Ed Kistner is a very kind-hearted man,*
> *To him you can always appeal.*
> *He goes and gets his corpses at very high speed*
> *Riding in his big automobile.*
> *Should you meet with death some dark night you feel*
> *And want an undertaker*
> *Ed Kistner will be at your home very quick*
> *For he goes in his big automobile.*
> *No matter how dark the night may happen to be*
> *Just telephone Ed Kistner and he will be there*
> *For he has light on his big automobile.*

A hint of eagerness in the verse, perhaps, but fittingly lugubrious. The following year, the *Valdosta Times*, another local American journal, carried an interesting personal ad shedding further light on the pioneer days of the smalltown mortician:

'This is to certify that I, Henry Rains, who was accused and arrested on a charge of selling poisoned whisky to W.A. Curry, undertaker, was found not guilty, because it was only embalming fluid which he asked me to bring him, and not poisoned whisky. I am making this statement to vindicate my name.'

Since those early days, the grander extravagances of the American way of death have become celebrated worldwide. In 1971, for example, the newspapers announced that the first high-rise mausoleum was to be built in Nashville Tennessee. The building was to be constructed in the shape of a cross. It would rise to some 300 ft, would be 20 storeys high, each storey carrying seven tiers of crypts. Occupying less than an acre of land, the mausoleum would provide 68,000 burial places. Engineers had carefully estimated the 'live weight' of the building; that is, its weight when in use. Nor had they forgotten that the average weight for a coffin and body is 350 lb, which decomposition reduces by nearly a half in a year.

High-rise mausoleums may be fairly commonplace by now, no longer possessing the power to amaze. (In 1929 *The Times* startled its readers with the headline: 'An Aerial Garage – Parking in the Skies'! The article went on to describe the first multi-storey car park in America.) Besides, no sooner had readers got used to Tennessee's extravaganza than Louisiana capped it with the world's first drive-in mausoleum.

The Point Coupee Funeral Home offered mourners the facility of viewing their dead relatives without leaving their cars. Visitors simply drove in and told the attendant the name of the loved one. Immediately, the dead relative beamed out through a seven foot drive-up window, displayed in an open casket and illuminated by blue neon light. The owner of the home said that people liked the relaxed atmosphere of the place so much that he had already rented it out for special occasions.

That was in 1977. Only one year later, came the Crunch. 'Will the Crunch Replace Cremation?' asked the *Sunday Times*, picking up on the latest American innovation in decorous death. The aim of this grisly form of burial was to reduce the body mass without cremation. To begin with, the corpse would be frozen rock solid by cooling in liquid nitrogen to $-100°C$. Next the frozen body would be 'pulverised in an automatic hammer until all chunks of bone, head, etc, do not exceed 13 millimetres'.

What could be more horrible? The final stage could be more horrible: in

---

Man in Coffin was Alive
Mr Douglas Gordon, aged 56, was taken to hospital in Nottingham last night after he had been seen to move in a coffin at an undertaker's mortuary.

He was given emergency treatment at the hospital after it had been confirmed that he was still alive.
The Times

**Victorian coffin
cupboard**

**Macabre coffin
cradle**

order to remove all traces of body fluids, 'the particles are reduced to 5 per cent their original weight by freeze-drying'.

How cosy the coffin by comparison. Sharon Morrison, manageress of the Rocky Mountain Casket Corp. in Montana found coffins so appealing that she began marketing them as articles of furniture which could be kept around the house until required for their final purpose. Her 'furniture caskets', made of three-quarter-inch knotty pine and fir sold for a modest £70 in 1974. The fittings, though, were extra, allowing the coffins to be converted into such items as wine racks, drinks cabinets, gun racks, billiard-cue racks and 'rustic coffee tables'. The most popular use, the manageress said, was as a wine rack.

The inventor of the convertible coffin was local attorney Willy Von Bracht who entered a local sports contest in a coffin toboggan of his own devising. However, he was well beaten by his own 11-year-old son in a rocking chair on skis.

Interestingly, the Rocky Mountain Casket Corp. was by no means the first company to market furniture caskets. The *Strand Magazine* of 1894 illustrates a precisely similar product called the coffin cupboard. The same magazine article also depicts what must surely be the most macabre item of domestic furniture of all time – a coffin cradle. A wooden crucifix supported the head of the cradle, with tinkling bells attached to comfort the unfortunate occupant. The item was clearly designed to instil awe of death at the earliest possible age.

Not everyone lives in fear of their own demise, however. Northamptonshire housewife Mrs Christine Farman held her own funeral party in July 1979. The 64-year-old grandmother told reporters: 'Like most families with old members we only seem to meet these days at each other's funerals. So I thought I'd hold my own funeral party while I am still around to enjoy it.'

She sent out invitations far and wide. Relatives turned up from places as distant as Canada. In fact, so many arrived that she had to hire out the village hall to accommodate them. It was wonderful: 'Now I'll die happy,' she said.

One person who missed the festivities, however, was Mrs Farman's 78-year-old husband, Percy. Percy overslept.

'He's a bit of an eccentric,' explained Mrs Farman.

R.I.P.
After 20 years of faithful service my vacuum cleaner gave out. I just didn't have the heart to put it out for the dustcart. Instead, I buried it at the end of the garden and planted a rose bush on top. I know this was daft, but it was the least I could do for such a helpful wee friend.
Letter in *Woman*

Remarkable Requests

When Mr Henry Cook, a prominent farmer from near Mayfield, Wellington, USA, accidentally fell beneath a tractor, the doctors advised an operation to remove his left leg, just below the hip. While he was coming out from under the influence of the anaesthetic he learnt that his relatives had made a remarkable request on his behalf. Believing that the injured man's soul might suffer if his whole person were not buried in hallowed ground, the relatives ordered a fine copper casket, 3 feet long, 14 inches wide and 10 inches deep to be prepared. It was lined with silk and in every respect other than size exactly resembled any other funeral casket. The leg was duly deposited in the casket, which was sealed airtight and properly disposed of. And so, long before his allotted span of years ended, Mr Cook had one foot in the grave.

The leg burial was a request of relatives. In other cases, those facing death have registered extraordinary last wishes on their own behalf. Take the case of Mrs Sandra West, aged 37, a Texas millionairess who died in March 1977. It was her desire to be buried in a lace nightgown in her favourite Ferrari car. The request caused considerable controversy and came before the courts in April of that year, when a judge ruled that her wish should be granted. And so, on 19 May the extraordinary burial took place at San Antonio in Texas. As requested, Mrs West was laid to rest 'with the seat slanted comfortably'.

A more modest wish was registered by Mr Kenneth James, a bachelor schoolteacher from Tower Hamlets in East London. His will stipulated that there was to be no funeral at all. His ashes were to be inconspicuously deposited 'in any convenient dustbin for refuse collection in the usual way'. Mr James died in May 1977, but his will was only published in September. The witness had not, of course, read the will, so they did not know about his last request. In the event, his ashes were quietly buried, with no relatives present, under a hydranga bed at an East London crematorium.

Complete Recovery Expected
Much improvement was shown in the condition of Diamond Joe Sullivan today, according to a physician's report, and his complete recovery is believed assured. When attendants report him completely out of danger, Governor McRae is expected to fix the day of his execution.
Little Rock Daily News

'We did not know of his wishes about the ashes,' said a spokesman. But at least Mr James was buried with anonymity.

Among all the bizarre requests which have been made, however, there can be none which surpass that of Mr André Tchaikowsky, who died at Cumnor in Oxfordshire in 1982. Tchaikowsky was an immensely gifted concert pianist (though no relation to the great Russian composer). And yet, the pianist's true ambition in life had been thwarted – he had always wanted to be an actor. Tchaikowsky died at the age of 46, in the summer of 1982. And he asked that after his death his skull should be given to the Royal Shakespeare Company for use in future productions of *Hamlet*.

After checking with the Home Office to make sure that it was not illegal, the task of removing the skull was left to the undertakers in Oxford. A partner in the firm told the press, 'Apparently he had a lifelong ambition to be an actor.' The skull was later delivered personally to the Royal Shakespeare Company, wrapped up in a box. 'We're somewhat bewildered by the whole business,' said a spokesman for the company. 'We'll store the skull away for the time being. As it happens, the company has no plans to stage *Hamlet* in the near future.'

Unquiet Graves

I n August 1982, the newspapers carried a macabre report from San Salvador, where the body of a man had been illegally exhumed by his own relatives. It appeared that a lottery ticket seller had arrived at the dead man's house to ask why he had not claimed his prize of $40,000. Further comment is hardly necessary – it is not hard to picture the frenzied excavations, the desperate scouring of pockets; but the ticket was not found.

Graves have often been disturbed over the centuries by occult practitioners, and body-snatching cases have made regular appearances in the press since the celebrated affair of Burke and Hare in 1828. William Burke was tried for participating in the murder of 16 victims, whose corpses were destined for the anatomist's table of a certain Dr Knox, who needed subjects for dissection. William Hare, Burke's accomplice in crime, was granted legal immunity for testifying against his companion.

The trial was a sensation, perhaps the first of the great 19th century crime block-busters, and the public were as ghoulish in their interest as any modern

William Burke, bodysnatcher

crowd. 'No trial that has taken place for a number of years past has excited such an unusual and intense interest,' recorded *The Times*. 'All the doors and passages to the court were besieged at an early hour before daylight, and it was with the greatest difficulty and the utmost exertions of a large body of police that admission could be procured for those who were concerned with the proceedings.'

No details were spared to readers, of the lugging of corpses and the doings to death, though reports were couched in the cumbersome language of the early 19th century courtroom. Of the death of Mary Paterson, for example, *The Times* faithfully recorded that Burke allegedly 'murdered Mary Paterson or Mitchell by placing or laying his body or person, or part thereof, over or upon the breast or person and face of Mary Paterson, when she was lying in the said house in a state of intoxication'. The prosecution then went on to charge him that 'by the pressure thereof, and by covering her mouth and nose with his body or person, and forcibly compressing her throat with his hands, and keeping her down, notwithstanding her resistance, did suffocate or strangle her'. It was by much the same method that one James Wilson 'commonly called Daft Jamie' was done to death.

William Burke was hanged in 1829, in front of 25,000 people in Edinburgh, and his infamous name has survived in the verb to 'burke' – meaning to smother or suppress. Hare, his accomplice, got off scot free.

A more haunting fear even than that of body-snatching, however, is the prospect of premature burial. In earlier ages, with less scrupulous medical practices than we enjoy today, the hazard of revival in coffin or grave was very real. During mass epidemics, especially, the bodies of the dead and dying were examined only cursorily if at all. Where Victorian graveyards have been opened up, clear evidence of premature burials has been revealed on a disturbing scale.

To counter quite justifiable fears of being buried alive, our forebears devised a number of ingenious contraptions. At the mid-19th century cemetery of Frankfurt-am-Main, for example, a room was set aside for corpses; strings were attached to the fingers of the bodies and these were connected to warning bells. A certain Count Karnice-Karnicki devised a graveyard apparatus which consisted of a $3\frac{1}{2}$ in tube, a sealed box, and a ball which lay on the chest of the deceased. At the slightest movement, a signal was set off above the ground, a door in the coffin sprang open and light and air were admitted.

As late as 1926, the *American Mercury* recorded that 'a telephone and electric lights have been stored in the mausoleum in which the body of Martin A. Sheets, stockbroker, was entombed. Sheets asked before his death that his tomb be so equipped that he might have opportunity to talk with the outside world if he should awaken in it.'

The Burial Reformer was issued in Britain from 1905–14, specifically to press for improvement in burial customs. Renamed *The Perils of Premature Burial* shortly after its inception, the magazine exposed such cases as the Accrington Sensation of January 1905, when a certain Mrs Holden, aged 29, was laid out as dead and prepared for entombment; the undertaker noticed a slight movement while completing his task, and revived the woman, who survived.

The magazine published a limerick popular at the time of the controversy:

> *There was a young man at Nunhead*
> *Who awoke in a coffin of lead;*
> *'It is cosy enough,'*
> *He remarked in a huff,*
> *'But I wasn't aware I was dead.'*

Despite all the advances of medical science, cases of corpses coming to life on morticians' slabs have persisted to the present day. Indeed, the practice of transplanting organs from the bodies of the newly dead has awakened the controversy afresh. *The Times* of 28 February 1976, for example, reported that a surgeon at a Birmingham hospital had described a 'dead' patient walking out of hospital having been rejected as a potential kidney donor. The patient was a middle-aged woman: 'Checks by experts showed no brain activity,' the surgeon said. Transplant surgeons had refused her body. She nevertheless recovered, and the surgeon had last seen her at an out-patient clinic.

The macabre experience of being buried alive was granted to Michael Baucom, aged 20, in 1982. Baucom was kidnapped, forced into a coffin and then buried under a Texas oilfield near Santa Fé. For four days he lay there in his underground tomb, with a little water, bread and a tube to breathe through. His parents tried to pay a $75,000 ransom, but the kidnappers failed to turn up to collect the money. The police, however, tracked them down and freed the kidnap victim, who survived.

Stranger still was the case of a 36-year-old Los Angeles man. As reported in the *Sun* of 14 September 1982, he managed to commit suicide by living burial in his own back garden. 'He even tried to pull a concrete slab over himself,' said police, who found hallucinatory drugs in a bedroom at his home.

Frozen Upright
A man was found in the Fleet Ditch standing upright and frozen to death. He appears to have been a barber at Bromley, Kent; had come to town to see his children, and had, unfortunately, mistaken his way in the night, and slipt into a ditch; and being in liquor could not disentangle himself.
The Gentleman's Magazine, 11 January 1763

DEATH & BURIAL

Charlie Chaplin's Vanished Corpse

Charlie Chaplin, the world's best-loved comic genius, died on Christmas Day 1977, and was buried two days later in a little cemetery overlooking Lake Geneva in Switzerland. He had spent his last 25 years in the nearby village of Corsier-sur-Vevey, where the comedian maintained a mansion. Throughout the world, newspapers published fulsome tributes to Chaplin's career both as actor and film director. His loss was genuinely felt.

And then, in the spring of 1978, while the tributes and anecdotes continued to flood in, a quite fantastic story broke. On 2 March, press reports from Lausanne announced that the body of Sir Charles Chaplin had vanished overnight from its grave at Corsier-sur-Vevey.

The cemetery was small and square, surrounded by a low stone wall. It stood at the end of a narrow lane on the edge of the village; the comedian's grave lay close to a wall near an avenue of tall, dark cypresses – it was just one among some 400 tombs mostly belonging to local people and marked by modest headstones and simple wooden crosses.

'The grave is empty. The coffin has gone,' a police official told reporters. At the Chaplin mansion in the village, a member of the domestic staff commented: 'Lady Chaplin is shocked. We all are. We can only wonder why – why should this happen to a man who gave so much to the world?'

Swiss police instituted a search and Interpol was brought in. Local people offered details which, in retrospect, might have alerted them to what had happened on the fateful night. One man said that shortly after midnight he had heard a noise like that of a pickaxe from the cemetery.

But who would want to steal the comedian's body? A number of theories were advanced in the days which followed. Since there had apparently been no ransom demand, one possibility was that the body might have been taken by a group of fanatical admirers. Frederick Sands, the author, had written a book about the Chaplins which referred to the comedian having once expressed a wish to be buried in England, the country of his birth. The investigating magistrate contacted the writer who told police that letters had been sent to him protesting about the burial in Switzerland. Had admiration for Chaplin really attained such heights that it amounted to cult worship?

Other theories concentrated on the fact that Chaplin was Jewish. A Hollywood report alleged that the body had been removed because Chaplin was buried in a Gentile cemetery.

Charlie Chaplin, film director

For a living film star to be kidnapped would be sensational enough. But Charlie Chaplin's corpse? The essential weirdness of the affair mystified both press and public.

Then, on 17 May, came the news that the kidnappers had been found – and the body recovered.

The culprits turned out to be two East European motor mechanics. By custom in Switzerland, first offenders are identified only by their initials, so the names of the mystery men were not announced at first; they quickly became known, however, to be Galtscho Ganev (a Bulgarian) and Roman Wardas (a Pole). The men had obtained political asylum in Switzerland some time earlier.

And the motive? It was ransom after all. Amid all the distressing press speculations, the Chaplins had had to keep silent to protect the police operation.

Briefly outlined, the kidnappers' story was that Wardas had got the idea for the body snatch when he read a newspaper report about a grave-robbing case in Italy. He was unemployed at the time, and going through a difficult period: 'As a result I decided to hide Charles Chaplin's body and solve my problems.' Wardas was the 'brains' behind the scheme (if such a term can be applied) and Ganev, his Bulgarian accomplice, was merely the muscleman.

During the night of 1 March they took two hours to dig out and remove the coffin from the Corsier cemetery. Then they loaded it into the back of an estate car and drove it just 15 miles to a cornfield at the eastern end of Lake Geneva. Wardas knew the spot because he had often gone fishing there. It took them an hour to dig a new grave. They inserted the coffin, took photographs and filled the grave in.

The two men waited for several weeks before telephoning the Chaplin family with ransom demands. At their trial it was revealed that they had used threats of violence against the family to try and secure a deal. Geraldine Chaplin, the comedian's actress daughter, had taken the calls because Lady Chaplin had been traumatized by the whole affair. Wardas had threatened to shoot Geraldine's younger brother and sister unless his demands were met.

But the kidnappers were, in reality, a sorry pair. They first asked for £330,000 then lowered the sum repeatedly over several calls until they were asking for £136,000. The police had been tapping the Chaplin's phone since the grave was robbed. The kidnappers announced that they would give instructions for the final ransom demand at 9.30 a.m. on a certain morning. That morning, the police kept watch on more than 200 telephone kiosks in the Lausanne area – Wardas was nabbed.

Wardas confessed at once when arrested, but would not reveal the identity of his partner in crime. The Bulgarian was quickly found, however, by checking up on the Pole's acquaintances. In fact, both 'brains' and 'muscle man' alike were so incompetent that when required by police to guide them to the burial site, they could not pinpoint exactly where they had hidden the coffin. Police officers had to use mine detectors.

The pair were convicted of disturbing the peace of the dead and of trying to extract a ransom. Wardas was sentenced to four and a half years of hard labour, while Ganev was given a suspended sentence of 18 months.

It had been a bizarre affair, as bizarre as any of the films which Chaplin had made. It had also been deeply distressing for the family. 'Instead of the love that centred round my father in the house, there was fear and threats,' said Geraldine Chaplin.

And the corpse? For all the supposed desires of Chaplin's elusive cult-worshippers, the comedian's remains were reburied in the same little cemetery at Corsier-sur-Vevey. The event had take place quietly, and before the trial. Only a few close friends and relatives were present at the simple graveside ceremony on 23 May 1978. As before, the body of Sir Charles Chaplin was laid to rest among the sad cypresses and modest crosses which overlook Lake Geneva.

But this time, the tomb was specially lined with concrete.

The Body Freezers – A Cryonic Shame

In the late 1960s, a book by Professor Robert Ettinger of Michigan fired the public imagination by suggesting that the bodies of the dead might be kept at sub-zero temperatures until medical science discovered a way to bring them back to life. The term 'cryonics' was coined for the concept. Particularly inspired by the book was a certain Robert Nelson, who founded a cryonics movement in the United States, offering to preserve the bodies of loved ones using just such methods.

Most scientists poured scorn on the scheme, but it provoked a whole spate of news stories. There was a particularly persistent rumour, for example, that Walt Disney, the millionaire animator, had been frozen and sealed in a cryonic chamber before his death.

Then, in May 1981, the world learned that all was not well in the immortality game. Take the case of Mildred A. Harris. She had been entered into suspended

animation on 12 September 1970, with a plaque reading: 'Today is the first day of your life.' Immediately the doctors had declared Mrs Harris to be legally dead, her relatives had got Robert Nelson's Cryonics Society of California to freeze her body and place it in a capsule. The Society indicated that it would keep the body at freezing temperature with a constant supply of liquid nitrogen as the preserving agent.

However, less than five years later, when Mrs Harris's sons checked the underground vault, they made a horrible discovery. Both their mother and father had been handed into the Society's safekeeping – and both bodies were badly decomposed.

Similar discoveries were made by two other families; the supplies of liquid nitrogen had been cut off.

As a result of their grim discoveries, the families joined cause and in 1981 sued the then defunct Cryonics Society of California and its founder for $10.5m (about £4.4m) damages, half a million dollars of which was claimed for emotional suffering. It was the first suit of its kind anywhere in the world, and it had very bizarre undertones.

In his defence, Robert Nelson stated that his Society had only been advertised as a super research company. Money paid to it was considered merely a donation. The organization had only promised to make the best possible effort to preserve the bodies (there were 15 in all) as long as it was practicable. The company ran out of money and could not afford to pay its bills. So the nitrogen supply was cut off.

The man who had offered immortality was working as a television repairman at the time of the court case.

The trial lasted several weeks, and its outcome in June 1981 was that Robert Nelson and an undertaker were ordered to pay some $1m in damages. Judgment on the broader claims of cryonics enthusiasts must remain suspended.

Beauty even in death – the body of this Inca boy was found in the Andes, preserved by natural agents for nearly 500 years. Low temperatures and lack of light, humidity and oxygen account for his near perfect condition.

Chapter Nine

The Ultimate Taboo

Bizarre human behaviour generally strikes us as weird because it offends some established convention, be it the dignity of death, the solemnity of religion, or merely some established code of acceptable conduct. If there is one convention which is almost universal, it is that eating people is wrong. Cannibalism may occur accidentally, for ritual purposes, for perverse satisfaction or the sheer needs of survival. But whatever the cause, reports of the practice touch something very deep in the human psyche. The subject is the ultimate taboo.

Who Shall we have for Dinner?

In 1973 there was a chronic meat shortage in Chile. One morning in February of that year, a labourer returned from an all-night drinking spree and delivered to his wife a 10 lb joint. How had he come by this unexpected delight? He told her he had been offered the meat at a bargain price in a Santiago street market. Without further ado, the wife set to work preparing a more than usually meat-rich stew.

The couple found that they had more meat than they needed, and the thrifty housewife sold some to her next door neighbour. This woman's suspicions were aroused, however, by the appearance of the meat. The skin and hair looked strangely human.

The two women took a package of meat round to their local police station. Their fears were confirmed – it was human flesh. Appalled by the discovery, the husband then admitted that he had not bought the meat, but had found the package lying on the ground.

A few days later, the trunk of a human body was found in a sack on the road to one of Santiago's cemeteries. It was soon proved to have belonged to the same individual as the 10 lb joint – they formed part of the dismembered corpse of an unknown murder victim.

Cannibalism inspires a horror perhaps exceeding any other human practice. Although the unwitting cannibalism of the Santiago couple is by no means unique, human flesh has generally been consumed for one of two reasons: to obtain perverse satisfaction, or to allay the peril of starvation.

There is an area in which the two motives meet – that of ritual cannibalism. Historians tend to believe, for example, that the Aztecs originally consumed the flesh of their enemies out of sheer necessity, to supplement a low protein diet. The practice then developed ceremonial overtones. The same may be true of certain African tribes and of New Zealand's Maoris.

The *Illustrated London News* of 21 May 1842 contains a curious account of a Maori arrested for being drunk and disorderly in Hoxton Square. The man turned out to be a Londoner born and bred, who had been kept a captive of cannibals for many years.

His name was Joshua Newborn, aged about 25, and his 'swarthy visage was tattooed like a native of New Zealand'; He had a strange tale to tell. Eleven years earlier he had been a boy on a whaler sailing the southern seas. The crew had fallen into the hands of the New Zealanders, and had all been captured and eaten by them. He had been reserved until last, but his life was spared when he agreed to live among them. Accordingly, he was given some narcotic and underwent the painful process of tattooing.

He lived among them for ten years altogether, often joining them in their battles with neighbouring tribes, and attending banquets in which prisoners were killed and eaten. Eventually, he had managed to escape and make his way home to England, where he was exhibited as a Maori chieftain at places of public amusement:

'A police constable of the N division stated, that while on duty at a late hour on Monday night, he heard an extraordinary kind of yelling in Hoxton Square, and proceeding to the spot, found the prisoner dancing about, and disturbing the neighbours with his wild and terrific cries. The prisoner, who was drunk, instead of desisting and going away as desired, set the witness and other constables at defiance, and after a violent resistance was lodged in the station-house.

Arrest of Joshua Newborn, 1842

THE ULTIMATE TABOO

'Serjeant Lambert said that he was exceedingly violent at the station-house, and vowed vengeance against the constable who took him there, threatening to feast upon his heart and "lick his chops with his blood"; and during the greater part of the night he appeared to be dancing his war dance in the cell, screeching at the top of his voice.

'The prisoner, whom the New Zealanders had named "Moika Makoura" the meaning of which he stated to be "The Tattooed Spirit", now expressed sorrow for his disorderly conduct. He very seldom drank spirits, but when he did, he said it made him quite wild.'

Cases of cannibalism for perverse satisfaction crop up in the newspapers. At the time of writing, for example, a man accused of cannibalism committed suicide in his cell in Poland; he was alleged to have murdered a woman, cut off her head, hands and feet and kept the torso, some of which he ate. In Hong Kong, meanwhile, three men were arrested after police discovered segments of women's bodies preserved in jars in their flat; cannibalism was suspected.

One of the most bizarre cases of recent years occurred in California, in July 1970, when two men were stopped by highway patrolmen near Big Sur. They had only been apprehended for a minor traffic offence. One, however, confided: 'I have a problem. I'm a cannibal.' He then confessed to murdering and eating a social worker.

Cannibalism practised out of sheer necessity comes into a very different category. Who can say with any confidence that they would not, if reduced by hunger to the pit of desperation, partake of human flesh? How can anyone, indeed, expect to understand the madness of starvation if in good health and well fed?

A German-born aviator put these questions directly to reporters in 1973. He was the pilot of a mercy mission aircraft which crashed in the Canadian Arctic wilderness. He was carrying three passengers: a pregnant Eskimo woman, her nephew, and a 27-year-old British nurse. The Beechcraft aeroplane crashed in a blizzard while on a 500-mile flight to take the nurse and her patients from Spence Bay to Yellowknife. David, the Eskimo boy, was suffering from suspected appendicitis and his aunt was in premature labour.

The nurse died in the crash, and the Eskimo woman two hours later. Both of the pilot's legs were broken. He and the boy managed to live for 20 days on a meagre supply of corned beef, sugar cubes, salt and soup. The boy built a shelter, provided firewood, and gathered lichens and mosses. As their condition weakened, the pair ate the frozen drugs in a medical bag and shared a one-inch piece of candle.

After 23 days, the boy died of starvation. At first the pilot wanted to die too, but then the will to live reawakened. 'I made a soup of lichens, no more than a spoonful,' he said later. 'I knew that since I could not get enough lichens to live,

I could not make it to the lake – 12 miles – to get fish. I needed food to fill the gap. From here on I think it is clear to everyone what I did. I'm still trying to forget this and probably will never succeed.'

The pilot began to eat the body of the nurse, and lived to survive his ordeal. He was rescued after spending 32 days in the frozen Canadian north. He admitted to his cannibalism soon after he was found by the Royal Canadian Mounted Police. At the inquest which followed, the nurse's parents stated that they bore no malice towards him.

The Hanover Vampire

'Nothing more revolting has been disclosed in the history of crime than the career of Fritz Haarmann, 44, known as the "Hanover Vampire"', declared the *News of the World*.

Haarmann, a black-marketeer, was brought to trial in Berlin in December 1924, and sentenced to death for 24 murders out of the 27 charged against him. All the victims were young men. His young accomplice, Hans Granz, was also ordered to be beheaded, but the sentence was subsequently commuted to 12 years' penal servitude. The details of Haarmann's atrocities were so dreadful that even the popular press glossed over certain aspects. *Reynolds's Illustrated Newspaper* noted: 'Suffice to say that Haarmann was a sexual degenerate, that he lured the boys into his house, and after giving a sumptuous meal he would praise the looks of his young guest. Then, later, in a room upstairs, the crime was committed.

'The end was always the same. Haarmann held his victim down and killed him with a bite in the throat. The monster's teeth held tight until the young life was gone.'

Even here the horror did not end. After World War One, many Germans lived close to starvation. Haarmann, like other black-marketeers, traded in meat of uncertain origin. The *News of the World* reported: 'All his victims were between 12 and 18 years of age, and it was proved that the accused actually sold the flesh for human consumption. He once made sausages in his kitchen, and, together with the purchased, cooked and ate them . . .'

For most of the ten-day trial, Haarmann was impassive. Once, the proceedings were held up so that the accused might smoke a cigar. It happened

---

Blood Pudding

During World War Two large amounts of human blood were collected from people willing to donate it to help casualties. So much blood was in fact given that there was something of a surplus.

Scientific advisers to the government, meanwhile, were worried about the nutritional requirements of the civilian population. They put forward a scheme to use the blood surplus as black pudding for distribution on the war ration.

The Ministry of Food eventually rejected the idea. Indeed, the proposal was only made public in November 1969, when Dr Magnus Pyke was giving a lecture to the Royal Institution in London on the subject of food and society. Pyke had himself been a scientific adviser during the war, and cited the rejection of the scheme as a 'striking example of the way in which food taboos can hamper good nutrition'.

It was interesting, he noted, that the British were quite prepared to consume each other's blood by vein – but considered taking it by mouth to be a variant of cannibalism.

---

while the mother of one of the victims was giving evidence; Haarmann was in such an obviously nervous state that the judge asked him if he needed anything. Haarmann requested a cigar to soothe his nerves and an usher was ordered to bring one.

The accused did not deny the murders – he was in no position to do so, for the evidence brought against him was overwhelming. But he claimed that they were all committed while he was in a state of trance. Hundreds of people had come in and out of his house quite safely. It was only when the irresistible urge came upon him that he went out and roamed the streets of Hanover to bring in a victim. He could not say what followed; he was not conscious when the atrocities were committed.

Afterwards, he cut up and disposed of the bodies of the boys. Their clothes were put on sale in the shop of an accomplice. Skulls were thrown into a river which ran to the back of his house.

Haarmann had taken extraordinary risks, and it was astonishing that suspicion did not fall on him earlier than it did. The whole of Hanover was alarmed by the disappearance of so many boys. How had he escaped detection? Some believed that Haarmann's meat trade was looked on indulgently by the police. Certainly, he had some connection with them; he acted as a police spy, and influential officials may have sheltered him when he first came under suspicion. Several members of the police force admitted that they had received

Peter Kurten, the Vampire of Düsseldorf, at his trial in 1930. A mass murderer like Haarmann, he admitted to 68 crimes of hideous bestiality. The sight of blood drove him to frenzy. As a boy he would cut the heads off swans to drink from their necks – later he graduated to humans. He drank from the throat of one female victim, and from the shattered forehead of another unfortunate. Kurten was beheaded in Cologne in July 1932.

gifts from him. In general, he was known as an obliging and pleasant-mannered man.

For the first few days of the trial, the evidence was given behind closed doors, 'being of too revolting a nature to find a place anywhere outside medical books', as *Reynolds's* put it. The monster's account of how he disposed of the bodies, however, was delivered in open court. Nearly 200 witnesses gave evidence, mostly parents and relatives of the murder victims: 'There were scenes of painful intensity as a poor father or mother would recognise some fragment or other of the clothing or belongings of their murdered son. Here it was a handkerchief, there a pair of braces, and again a greasy coat, soiled almost beyond recognition, that was shown to the relatives and to Haarmann. And with the quivering nostrils of a hound snuffling his prey, as if he were scenting rather than seeing the things displayed, did he admit at once that he knew them.'

If Haarmann was a psycopath, what of Granz, his accomplice? The man emerged in the trial as a sinister figure whose motives were shadowy. Cynical, callous, he drove the victims into Haarmann's room and he clearly knew what was happening there. On one occasion, Haarmann was going to release a victim – Granz drove the boy back to slaughter.

There were some clues to Haarmann's own mental condition; in particular, a driving hatred of his father seemed to have been a dominant obsession. Haarmann did not, however, use insanity in his defence. On the contrary, he implored his judges not to send him to an asylum. He had been confined to prisons and mental hospitals during his earlier days, and did not want the experience repeated. In fact, time after time, he appealed that the trial be ended quickly so that he could be put to death.

The close of the trial was sensational. A fanatic had sworn that he would shoot the murderer as soon as sentence was pronounced so that no opportunity for clemency could be exercised. Every member of the public who came into court was carefully searched for weapons. Expecting a fatal shot at any moment, the judges were protected by a row of policemen watching for the slightest movement in the gallery. Though the threat heightened the courtroom drama, however, the fanatic did not make his attempt.

Concluding his own address, Haarmann pleaded:

'Condemn me to death. I only ask for justice. I am not mad. It is true that I

Fangs for the Memory
A call girl in Malagasy who wore vampire-like teeth to frighten clients into fleeing without their wallets, has been arrested.
Sun

---

often get into a state of which I know nothing, but that is not madness. Make it short, make it soon. Deliver me from this life which is a torment. I will not petition for mercy, nor will I appeal. I have made things easy for you gentlemen; make them also easy for me. I should like to add that the police have done everything possible to clear up the affair. At first I denied, but they started rather roughly with me, and that I cannot bear. Afterwards the situation became clear to me and it is still absolutely clear. I thank you gentlemen.'

When the sentence of death had been pronounced, the doomed man asked that the following inscription should be inscribed on his tombstone: 'Here rests the mass murderer, Haarmann'.

He also expressed a desire to pass 'one merry evening' in his cell. His last meal should consist of coffee, hard cheese and cigars, after which he would curse his father and regard his execution as his wedding.

The Raft of the Medusa

T he most famous historical episode, in which survivors of a shipwreck have been reduced to cannibalism, followed the loss of the French frigate *Medusa*. Contemporaries were haunted by the grim narrative, much as present-day newspaper readers have been by the case of the Andes survivors. The raft is the subject of a celebrated painting by Géricault, which hangs in the Louvre in Paris. The artist has conferred a kind of tragic dignity upon his subject – a dignity not felt by the survivors themselves. The following account is based on the report of the ship's surgeon, which appeared in the *Journal des Débats*, and was reproduced in *The Times* of 17 September 1816.

The *Medusa* was wrecked off the African coast on 2 July that year. Besides the crew of seamen there were many soldiers and officers on board. The ship went down slowly, and there was time both to organize boats and to build a raft of masts and yardarms.

The original intention was to place supplies on the 60 ft raft, and to tow it with the boats. Measures of flour, barrels of wine and casks of water were set up, and only ten men put aboard at first. Others soon clambered on, however, and the raft sank low in the water. A case of biscuit was thrown down from the frigate; it fell into the sea but was eagerly retrieved, its contents reduced to a

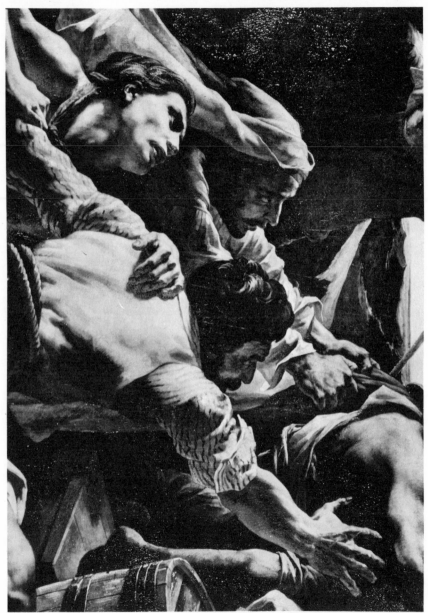

Detail of Gericault's *Raft of the Medusa*

A Tale of the Frozen North
They breed 'em tough in the Yukon Territory; smart too. A toothless trapper named Nimrod Robertson once shot a bear. How to cope with its sinewy flesh? Robertson hacked into the creature's mouth and extracted the wherewithal to make a denture. He then ate the bear with its own teeth.

sodden paste. In all, 147 men crowded onto the hastily prepared vessel, so that they stood waist deep in water. The provisions of flour were jettisoned – and the plan of towing the raft was abandoned.

The *Medusa* sank beneath the waves, and despite the distress of the men on the raft, the ship's boats disappeared over the horizon. That night, 20 of the raft's occupants died, swept away by the sea or trapped underwater with their legs caught between the planks. Throughout the whole of the next day, the survivors' spirits were sustained by the hope that the boats would return – but they never did. By nightfall, depression had set in, and it deepened when the sky darkened and a storm blew up.

The most determined survivors fought their way to the centre of the raft. All who failed were lost to the tossing waves, while others were crushed to death in the struggle.

The next day, mutiny broke out. Soldiers and sailors gave way to despair and broke open the casks of wine, drinking themselves into a frenzy. Some tried to sever the cords which bound the raft together, and to make off on their own. One rebel was cut down by an officer with a sabre, and a pitched battle broke out on the waterlogged craft. Some of the rebels advanced with knives; those without weapons 'endeavoured to tear us with their teeth: many of us were cruelly bitten,' the surgeon recalled. 'I was so myself in the legs and on the shoulder.'

The officers formed ranks and slashed back with their sabres, receiving help from loyal crewmen. 65 men, mostly mutineers, were slaughtered in the battle, some having hurled themselves into the sea in despair. When at last the fighting ended, it was found that the water casks had been lost, and that only one cask of wine remained. A strict system of rationing was introduced, and was greeted with bitter resentment. It was then that thoughts of cannibalism occurred.

'I shudder with horror while I retrace that which we put into practice,' wrote the surgeon. 'I feel my pen drop from my hand: a mortal coldness freezes all my limbs, and my hair stands on end. Great God!'

Survivors of the battle threw themselves onto the dead bodies which littered the raft. In some cases, slices were cut from the corpses and devoured on the spot. Some survivors resisted the temptation at first, but most succumbed later.

The surgeon himself proposed drying the bleeding limbs to 'render them a little more supportable to the taste'. A few men abstained completely, and were granted extra rations of wine in compensation. When order was restored after the first orgy of consumption, all corpses but one were thrown overboard, the last being 'destined to feed us'.

As the fourth night approached, a little miracle occurred. A shoal of flying fish got trapped under the raft and hundreds were taken aboard. That evening a bizarre banquet was held. A fire was made from the debris of a barrel lit with gunpowder, and on it the ravenous survivors cooked a mixed grill of broiled flying fish and roasted human flesh.

On the fifth night, another mutiny broke out. When day broke there were only 30 survivors left. The salt water had scoured the skin from their lower legs and covered their bodies with stinging wounds and contusions. Twelve fish remained, with enough wine to last only four days on strict rationing. Then, two soldiers were found to be sucking wine from the last cask by means of a long straw. They were knifed and thrown into the waves.

Thirteen of the remaining men were so sick and delirious that their hopes of survival were reckoned to be slight. Moreover, they were using up rations which might possibly save others. With heavy hearts, the healthier survivors resolved that they must die. Three seamen and a soldier took upon themselves the responsibility of executing the unfortunates, and after this grim procedure, all weapons were thrown overboard in disgust.

'Our minds were soured,' wrote the surgeon. 'Even in the arms of sleep our imaginations depicted the mangled limbs of our unfortunate companions, and we invoked death with loud cries. A burning thirst, redoubled by the rays of a fiery sun, consumed us: it was such that our parched lips sucked with avidity the urine which we endeavoured to cool in small tin vessels.'

And so the days passed for the 15 remaining survivors. 'We despised life to such a degree that several of us were not afraid to bathe even in sight of the sharks which surrounded our raft.' For the flesh which they had devoured so eagerly before, they began to experience only disgust.

And then, on the twelfth day of the grim ordeal, the mast of a ship was sighted on the horizon. Elated, the survivors piled up empty casks topped by an array of multicoloured handkerchiefs in order to attract its attention. The ship disappeared. From delirious joy, the men passed to deepest despair. 'For myself,' wrote the surgeon, 'I envied the fate of those whom I had seen perish at my side.' Two hours later, however, the ship was sighted again, less than a third of a league off, and coming towards them in full sail. Bearded and hollow-eyed, half-naked and festering with hideous sores, the 15 survivors wept uncontrollably as the French brig *Argus* drew near and they heard their countrymen calling to them from the deck. The long ordeal was over.

The Andes Survivors

As far as the outside world was concerned they were dead. Stranded in a wrecked fuselage high amid the Andes, the members of a Uruguayan rugby club had a choice: they could starve to death or eat the flesh of friends whose bodies lay scattered in the snow around. Sixteen chose to live, and their tale is as heroic as it is bizarre.

On 12 October 1971, 45 Uruguayans left Montevideo for Santiago in a twin-engined Fairchild. Most were young men, and members of the Old Christians rugby club. Their team had finished second in the Uruguayan league and was now off to play a match in Chile. After the game there would be a few days of skiing in a Chilean mountain resort. Some members had mothers and sisters with them. They were looking forward to the holiday.

The 'plane belonged to the Uruguayan Air Force, and the flight was delayed because of bad weather in the Andes. But on 13 October, the aircraft set off again. High above the mountains, however, a blizzard set in. The 'plane hit an air pocket, jolted and went into a dive with its engines screaming. And for months which followed, all that the world knew was that the aircraft had disappeared.

On board the plane, however, an appalling ordeal was beginning. The aircraft plunged some 3,000 feet in a matter of seconds. Snowy crags were glimpsed not six feet from the wing tip; and then the plane dived again, smashing against a mountainside, its tailplane wrenched off to career down the slope.

'People who failed to get their seat belts fastened were simply swept out of the hole left when the tail broke off,' a survivor named Inciarte later recalled in a *New York Times* report from which much of the following material is drawn. 'Blood spurted all over me, people were screaming and I could smell fuel and the cold air gushing in from outside, when suddenly with one big bump we came to rest.'

The aircraft lay amid mountains rising to 21,000 feet, in a place as desolate and remote as an Antarctic waste. The pilot was dead in the wreckage. Sixteen others lay dead or dying around, including all the women passengers.

Staggering to their feet amid the carnage, the 28 survivors felt the bite of the sub-zero temperature. But at least they did not perish overnight through the cold, for they had with them the warm skiing clothes they had brought for the projected holiday. Those clothes, and the fitness of the young club members, were to prove crucial in the months of suffering which followed.

There was also a transistor radio, though it had no batteries. The only

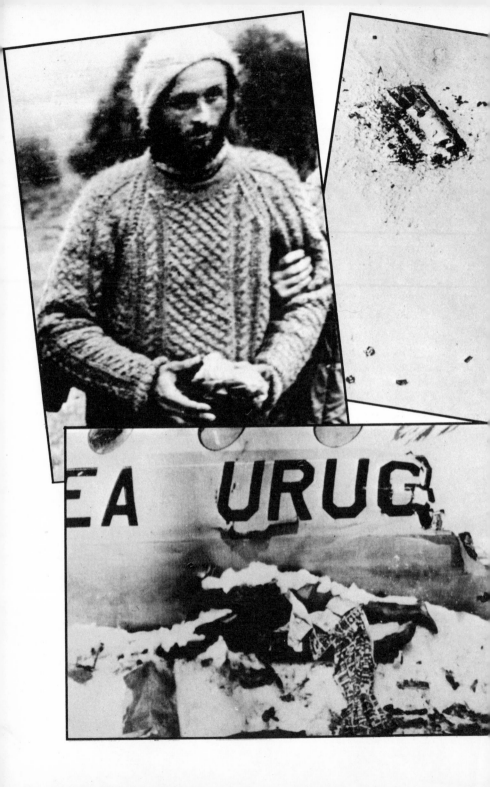

Far left: Fernando
Parrado
Left: The plane
wreckage in the snow
Below left: Victims of
the crash
Below: Survivors
attend mass

surviving member of the aircrew declared that batteries were stored in the tailplane. It was two miles away. An expedition was mounted to retrieve them, but they were found to be too heavy to move. Instead, the radio was taken to the tailplane and attempts were made to rig up a transmitter for signalling distress. After many days of struggling with numb fingers, however, the attempts failed. Nonetheless, it did prove possible to set up a receiver, and the group was able to listen to radio broadcasts from Montevideo.

Powerless to guide or inform, the Andes survivors heard of search parties and rescue squads scouring the mountains for signs of the vanished aircraft. With every day that passed, the hopes of the searchers grew fainter. And at midday on 21 October, the survivors heard the news they were dreading. The search parties had been called off. The Chilean Mountain Rescue Service announced that attempts to find the plane would resume during the spring thaw. No one, it was thought, could have survived in that temperature and in that terrain.

And yet the group had survived. At one end of the wrecked fuselage, the partially destroyed cabin offered some insulation against the bitter cold. At the open end, an assortment of partitions was erected. The aircraft had settled into the snow up to window level. It was hardly snug – but it sheltered the group against the worst of the elements.

Covers were ripped from seats and converted into blankets. Some people slept in hammocks composed of cable and cord. Others slept on metal plates laid at an angle against the wall; they developed sores on the backs of their necks from lying night after night in the same position.

They slept as close to each other as they could to keep warm, and the restless tossing of one might graze the chapped limbs of another. But there were few serious quarrels. Team spirit, as much as fitness, played its part in sustaining the rugby club members during their long ordeal.

At first, the survivors had tried to eat snow for water. Severe cramps ensued from the cold. Later, aluminium sheets from the plane were propped up to provide a solar melting device. Snow piled up on top warmed and dripped into bottles placed underneath.

Such solid food as had been stored in the aircraft was gradually exhausted however. And as the days passed, and the pangs of hunger grew stronger, the decision to consume flesh from the bodies of dead companions was taken.

The choice was not easy to make. In Catholics, a sense of sacrilege is deeply felt. But so too is a sense of the sacrament. The group shared the flesh of their companions as Christ Himself had shared His body.

Not everyone chose to accept the decision. One survivor, Numa Turcatti, considered the toughest and fittest of the group, suddenly lost heart in the business. He was given food but he hid it and threw it away when the others were not looking. Turcatti simply let himself die.

A victim is recovered from the snow

Fernando Parrado rescued after his 10-day trek to civilization

But those who had determined to survive at all cost took precautions as sensible as those applied to the fitting out of the fuselage. Strips of flesh were cut up and left to hang until ready for consumption. A rationing system ensured that each corpse should last the survivors five days. Nobody feasted with relish. The flesh was consumed in small pellets to minimize the ordeal of chewing. The madness of starvation remained close at hand, and everyone experienced hallucinatory dreams of fantastic banquets. Once, the survivors drew up a list of the best restaurants in Montevideo to while away the hours of numb despair.

On 29 October a fresh disaster struck, further reducing the group's number. An avalanche bore down on the aircraft, wrecking their living quarters as tons of compacted snow churned through the fuselage. Nine lives were lost.

From the outset, group members had made small foraging expeditions when taking the daily trips to the radio in the tailplane. All movement was slow in the thin air, but sometimes an excursion brought a reward. One big find was a packet of 170 cigarettes fallen from the plane as it burst apart. After the avalanche, however, the survivors felt more strongly than ever how precarious their existence was; it was clear that someone should at least try to reach help.

Three men were selected for the expedition. To equip them for the intense cold, the group pried felt covers from heating tubes in the aircraft, fashioning them into bands to be wrapped round the men's bodies.

Of the three who set out, one turned back after three days in order to save rations. The two who continued were Parrado, a burly rugby forward, and Canessa, a third-year medical student who had become the group's doctor. On leaving, Parrado had promised: 'Before Christmas I will have you out of here.'

The feat which the two men accomplished was an epic of endurance. With their improvised clothing, they scaled heights which had not been attempted before by fully equipped mountaineers. 'We had no idea where we were going,' Canessa recalled, 'but with the aircraft compass we had to get there. Chile was to the west and we would go there whatever happened. So we started those unending days of travel – intense cold at night, intolerable heat at midday. We rationed the water and food and I said: "If we don't walk so far, then no food for us."'

It was Parrado, however, whose extraordinary stamina and determination proved the most enduring. Towards the end he was carrying his companion.

At 9 p.m. on 20 December, a 44-year-old cattle hand from San Fernando was tending his herds in the foothills of the Andes. He heard faint cries from across the River Tinguiririca, a rushing torrent which carves its way through the mountains' lower slopes. On the other side he saw what seemed to be two tramps. The roaring water drowned the men's shouting – he had his cattle to look after and night was falling. He shouted that he would return the next day.

The following morning, the tramps were still there, and still the torrent muffled their cries. The cattle hand threw over a piece of paper and a pencil attached to a stone. The message which was hurled back read:

'I come from the plane that crashed in the mountains. I am Uruguayan. We have been walking like this for 10 days. My friend is injured. There are still 14 injured people on the plane. We have to get out of here quickly because we have nothing to eat. We can walk no more.'

The cattle hand rushed off to find help, but it was midnight before patrols reached the pair.

Meanwhile there was a jubilation in the wrecked fuselage. The survivors had learnt by radio that Parrado and Canessa had got through. The arduous discipline of maintaining the aircraft had been abandoned. The last remaining cigarettes had been rolled into huge cigars.

By the afternoon of 22 December, most of the survivors had been rescued by teams of mountaineers supported by helicopters. Those who first reached the scene were astonished to find human limbs scattered outside the aircraft, and strips of flesh hanging inside ready for consumption. Neither Parrado nor Canessa had spoken of what had passed in the mountains. Indeed, the earliest press reports described the survivors as having lived on lichens. The experts, however, knew that this could not be true. The survivors were too fit and too lucid. The full story emerged only later.

Bad weather prevented the last batch of survivors from being taken off the mountain until 23 December – the day after their companions. It is not hard to imagine the mixed euphoria and anxiety of the little group huddled in the lonely hulk during that last night in the Andes. All were freed nevertheless.

In total, the Uruguayans' ordeal had lasted 70 days. But Parrado had kept to his promise – he got them all out by Christmas.

PDO 83-278